LEAD WITH PURPOSE

LEAD WITH PURPOSE

A STORY ABOUT LEADING IN YOUR PERSONAL AND PROFESSIONAL LIFE

Dr. Kevin McGarry

Illustrated by Madison McGarry

Lead with Purpose

A Story About Leading In Your Personal And Professional Life

McGarry Leadership
Avon, CT
www.mcgarryleadership.com

Hardback ISBN: 979-8-9909338-0-4
Paperback ISBN: 979-8-9909338-1-1
EBook ISBN: 979-8-9909338-2-8
Library of Congress Control Number: 2024912880

Editing and Interior Design: Self-Publishing Genie
www.selfpublishinggenie.com

To my wife, Kristen, and my daughter, Madison. Kristen, your passion for everything you do and the resulting success is an inspiration to our family. Madison, may your softball field of dreams extend to every corner of your life. This book is dedicated to the extraordinary women who make my world shine.

CONTENTS

LEAD WITH PURPOSE

CHAPTER 1

Unspoken Tensions

"A life with love will have some thorns, but a life without love will have no roses."

—Dr. Seuss

The suburban twilight cast a warm glow on the façade of Eddie Mitchell's home as he turned the key in the front door. The familiar creak of the hinges echoed through the quiet hallway, signaling the end of another demanding day as a sales manager at Aerospace Technologies. The weight of the day's challenges of an unmotivated sales team and sluggish sales lingered on his shoulders as he stepped through the familiar threshold of his serene suburban home.

A snapshot of disconnection unfolded before him. In the living room, seated upon the worn upholstery of the couch, was Riley, his teenage daughter, her slender frame enveloped by the soft glow of her cell phone. The gentle light cast upon her features, illuminating the delicate curve of her jawline and the flow of chestnut hair framing her face with freckles scattered across her cheeks. The once-vibrant girl who used to eagerly share stories from school and giggle over dinner had become a mere silhouette, lost in the digital abyss.

Erin, Eddie's wife, moved about the kitchen, stirring a pot on the stove, her mind occupied by more than just the evening meal. Her dark-brown eyes, however, were not fixed on the stove or the ingredients but rather on her cell phone, a conduit to the world of local community drama consuming her thoughts. The incessant jabbering of a group chat with other mothers had become a constant companion, filling the void left by the almost nonexistent conversations with her husband.

The home, once echoing with laughter, conversations, and shared dreams, hummed with an undercurrent of unspoken tensions. The living room, adorned with family photographs frozen in moments of joy, now held an air of detachment. Eddie felt lost on how to bring everything back to where they were only a few short years ago.

"Eddie, you're home," Erin greeted him, her voice a strained attempt at normalcy. Her eyes, however, barely lifted from the screen, as her brown hair fell loosely around her face while she tended to a simmering pot, a clear indication her attention was divided between cooking and the unfolding neighborhood drama. With a distracted gesture, she absentmindedly tucked a stray lock of hair behind her ear.

"Hey, sweetheart," Eddie replied, his voice carrying a hint of weariness. He moved toward the living room, eyeing

Riley, who offered him a brief glance before returning to her digital world.

"How was your day?" Erin asked, her words almost automatic, a token inquiry lacking the genuine curiosity of someone eager to connect.

"Long," Eddie admitted, taking a seat on the couch opposite Riley. He glanced at the digital divide between them: the glowing screen holding his daughter's attention and the virtual world seeming to captivate his wife.

Eddie sighed inwardly, feeling like a visitor in his own home. The family photographs of birthday parties, lake weekends, and trips to Europe seemed like yesterday. Yet today, any attempts at conversation were met with fragmented responses, as though the invisible barriers of distraction had rendered genuine connection an elusive feat.

As Eddie settled into the couch to check the score of the Yankees game, he could not shake the feeling the home to which he returned to each evening was slipping away, transforming into a landscape of disconnected routines and unspoken frustrations. Little did Eddie know this seemingly ordinary evening would become the precursor to a journey challenging not only the dynamics within his home but also the very threads binding the family together.

CHAPTER 2

Boardroom to the Bleachers

"Opportunities multiply as they are seized."

—Sun Tzu

Erin called out, "Dinner's ready, everyone!" Her invitation echoed into the living room, reaching the ears of both Eddie and Riley. The clattering of utensils and the soft hum of conversation should have followed, creating an ambiance of familial connection. However, as the family gathered around the table, an unspoken tension settled in the room, like a heavy fog.

As Riley continued to scroll through her phone, Eddie couldn't help but feel a sense of discontent. The dinner table, once a place of shared stories and laughter, had become a disjointed space where each family member inhabited a separate sphere of existence.

Riley, with her phone clutched in hand, took her seat nonchalantly, her attention tethered to a digital world existing beyond the kitchen. Eddie, once the jovial center of family conversations, sat in muted silence, his thoughts focused on the challenges at Aerospace Technologies with an occasional glance drifting toward the family photo on the wall—a frozen moment of happiness that felt distant from the present reality.

Erin, despite her efforts to initiate conversation, found herself met with one-word responses and fleeting eye contact. The once-vibrant atmosphere accompanying family dinners had transformed into a few disconnected individuals sharing a meal in silence.

The strains of unspoken words and unresolved tensions lingered, casting a shadow over what should have been a simple family meal. The disconnect, more profound than the physical space between them, painted an intricate portrait of a family navigating the complexities of their individual worlds, each member a solitary figure within the confines of the dinner table.

Just as everyone finished their meal, the phone rang, cutting through the uneasy silence. Eddie instinctively reached for the device, a subtle knot of anxiety tightening in his stomach. In a life dictated by conference calls, sales targets, and corporate demands, a ringing phone often came with another pressing issue at work—an urgent matter demanding his immediate attention.

As Eddie glanced at the screen, the name "Lisa" illuminated in bold letters; a wave of relief washed over him. Lisa, Riley's softball coach, was a familiar presence in his life—a connection to a world beyond the corporate chaos often consuming him. The tension in his shoulders eased slightly as he answered the call, hoping this conversation would offer a welcome respite from the challenges of corporate sales management.

"Hey, Lisa," Eddie greeted, his voice a touch more animated than it had been throughout the evening.

"Hi, Eddie. I hope I'm not interrupting anything important." Lisa's voice held a note of concern, as if she could sense the strained atmosphere through the phone.

"No, not at all. What's going on?" Eddie replied, glancing briefly at the remnants of the family dinner. The unspoken tension lingered in the air, making the prospect of a conversation with Lisa a welcome diversion.

There was a momentary pause on the line, and then Lisa began with a weighty urgency. "Eddie, we're in a tight spot. We've lost our head coach unexpectedly, and the other assistant coach had to step down. The next game is just a week away, and we're short-staffed. The girls really look up to you, and I can't think of anyone better to step into the role. I have assumed the role of head coach; would you consider being the assistant coach for the rest of the season?"

Eddie's gaze shifted from the phone to a photo of Riley's T-ball team, which had been proudly displayed for the last four years on the kitchen counter. Eddie, the coach, stood next to Riley, both with huge smiles—a frozen moment of happiness that seemed distant from the current reality. The request to join as assistant coach pulled at the threads of his past, connecting him to a time when the diamond was not just a distant memory.

Outside of coaching Riley's T-ball team, it had been years since Eddie had set foot on a baseball field, the place where his love for the game had begun. Back then, he was a star athlete, a natural leader on and off the field. The sound of a fastball hitting a catcher's mitt and the cheers of the crowd had been the rhythms of his life. Victory had been his constant companion and the diamond his sacred ground.

But life had a way of leading him down a different path. Eddie had traded his baseball dreams for a suit and tie, chasing promotions and climbing the corporate ladder. As the demands of his career had grown, his connection to the sport he loved had faded. The field had become a distant memory, and the crack of a bat seemed like a relic of the past.

As Lisa continued to explain the situation, Eddie felt a flicker of excitement amidst the chaos of his personal and professional life. The prospect of rekindling a connection with Riley through softball, of stepping onto the field once more, seemed like a lifeline in the midst of the challenges he faced.

Eddie's initial response was hesitant. His role leading a sales team demanded his full attention, and his sales team was facing challenging times. The thought of adding coaching to his already packed schedule was daunting. He was used to working late into the night, strategizing deals and navigating the ever-evolving world of sales.

"Lisa, I . . . I appreciate the offer," Eddie finally spoke, his voice undecided. "Let me discuss it with Erin and Riley and get back with you."

The glow from Eddie's phone gradually dimmed as he ended the call with Lisa. He turned to face Erin, who was clearing the dinner table with a practiced efficiency. The unspoken tension in the room lingered, casting a subtle shadow over the prospect of Eddie taking on the role of assistant coach for Riley's softball team.

"Eddie," Erin began, her voice measured, "what was that call about? Everything okay?"

Eddie took a deep breath, the weight of the decision he was about to share settling on his shoulders. "That was Lisa, Riley's softball coach. They're in a tough spot. They lost their head coach, and the assistant coach had to step down. Lisa asked if I would consider being the assistant coach for the rest of the season."

Erin paused in her movements, her eyes meeting Eddie's with a mix of curiosity and concern. "Softball coach? Eddie, you're already swamped with work, and you've been talking about the challenges with your team. Can you really add coaching to the mix?"

Eddie ran a hand through his hair, his gaze drifting to the T-ball team photo. "I know, Erin. It's just . . . it's a tough situation. The girls need someone who knows the game, and Lisa thinks I can make a difference. Plus, it's a chance to spend more time with Riley."

Erin sighed, her shoulders slumping. "Eddie, I get that spending time with Riley is important, but you're already working late into the night. The pressure at work is intense, and we barely get any time together as a family. Adding coaching to the mix, especially now, might make things even more challenging."

Eddie nodded, acknowledging the validity of Erin's concerns. "I know it's a lot, Erin. But the field used to be my sacred ground, you know? I miss being a part of something beyond work, beyond the corporate chaos. And Riley . . . she loves softball. I feel like I'm missing out on something important in her life."

Erin placed a hand on Eddie's shoulder, a gesture of understanding. "Eddie, I get it. I really do. But we're a team too. Your work, our family, us—it's all interconnected. If you take on coaching, it's going to impact all of that. Are you sure you can handle it, especially with everything else going on?"

Eddie met Erin's gaze, his crystal-blue eyes reflecting a mix of determination and uncertainty. "I want to do this, Erin. For Riley, for myself, for the family. It's a chance to reconnect with something I love, to be there for our daughter. But I also don't want it to strain us even more. What do you think?"

Erin sighed, the weight of the decision apparent in her expression. "Eddie, I want you to be there for Riley too. And you know, coaching might give you some purpose back in your life. If it's something you truly want and believe in, maybe it's worth exploring. Just talk to Lisa about the time commitment and see if there's a way to make it work without overwhelming yourself."

Eddie nodded, grateful for Erin's perspective. "You're right, Erin. I'll talk to Lisa and figure out the details. I don't want it to be another source of stress. We'll find a way to make it work for everyone."

With a quick call back to Lisa accepting the role as assistant coach to the Blue Lightning, Eddie's journey back to the diamond began. Little did he know his return to coaching would not only bridge the gap between his corporate life and his love for the game but also lead him down a path of unexpected leadership lessons and personal growth. As he hung up the phone, he couldn't help but wonder where this new adventure would take him.

CHAPTER 3

Humbling Revelation

"Humility is to make a right estimate of oneself."
—Charles H. Spurgeon

Eddie Mitchell stood on the softball field, a furrowed brow betraying his frustration. His eyes followed the team as they fumbled through yet another lackluster practice. Doubt gnawed at him, not only about his coaching abilities but also about his leadership skills in the corporate world.

Lisa, the head coach, had been struggling to motivate the girls with her pep talks and instructions. The players with blank facial expressions appeared disinterested, much like Eddie's sales team when he attempted to inspire them during morning meetings. As he observed Lisa's efforts, a troubling thought began to form in his mind: perhaps neither of them was an effective coach or leader.

After practice, Eddie approached Lisa with a hesitant smile. "Lisa," he began, "I've been doing some thinking, and

I can't help but notice that we're facing similar challenges in our roles as coaches."

Lisa's subtly elongated face tightened, her frustration evident. Eddie pressed on. "Let's take a closer look at what's not working. In softball, I've noticed that the girls lack motivation. They seem disengaged and unresponsive to our instructions and pep talks. It's like they're going through the motions without any real passion for the game."

Lisa's frustration deepened, and she shot Eddie a piercing look with her hazel eyes. "Eddie, this isn't just about noticing things. I've been coaching these girls for a while now. I know the challenges we're facing, and it's not as simple as a lack of passion. We're dealing with different personalities, skill levels, and expectations. It's a complex puzzle, and I've been trying my best to piece it together."

Eddie hesitated, realizing his attempt to draw parallels might not have been well received. "I didn't mean to oversimplify, Lisa. I just think we need to reevaluate our approach. The last time I coached was T-ball and directing the players worked because they were so young; this team is different, the girls have advanced. Maybe there's a way to connect with the girls on a deeper level, to inspire them in a way that resonates with each of them individually."

Lisa crossed her arms, her frustration giving way to a defensive stance. "Eddie, coaching is more than just strategy and inspiration. It's about understanding each player's unique strengths and challenges. It's about adapting our coaching style to bring out the best in every individual on the team. I've been trying to do that, but it's not as straightforward as it sounds."

Eddie nodded, realizing that their perspectives on the coaching challenges were diverging. "I get that, Lisa. Maybe I'm approaching this from a different angle because of my background, but I genuinely believe that there's untapped potential in each player. We just need to find the right way to unlock it."

Lisa's eyes narrowed, a subtle tension building between them. "Eddie, coaching is not a one-size-fits-all solution. We can't just apply the same strategies to everyone and expect magic to happen. It's about understanding and adapting, yes, but it's also about managing expectations and being realistic about what we can achieve."

Eddie paused, contemplating a new approach. "I think it's time for me to take a step back and learn how to be a better coach and leader myself. I've been doing some research, and there's a lacrosse coach and corporate leader I know, Mark Turner. He's had remarkable success in both fields, and I believe he can offer us valuable insights. I'm going to reach out to him and see if he'd be willing to mentor me. I'll bring back the lessons I learn from him, which we can implement in both coaching and leadership."

Lisa was intrigued. "That sounds like an interesting idea, Eddie. Mark Turner is a local legend in lacrosse; it would be interesting to hear his perspective, and his expertise could be just what we need to coach this team."

Eddie smiled, feeling a renewed sense of purpose. "Exactly, Lisa. Let's commit to becoming better leaders and coaches together. Once I've gained insights from Mark, we'll work together to inspire our softball players."

As they left the softball field that day, Eddie felt a sense of determination. Acknowledging the challenges of coaching and leadership was a difficult but necessary step toward growth. He hoped that by embarking on this journey of self-improvement and learning from a successful lacrosse coach like Mark Turner, they could transform their coaching styles and inspire both their softball team and his sales team to achieve greater success.

CHAPTER 4

Sips of Wisdom

"An investment in knowledge always pays the best interest."
—Benjamin Franklin

Eddie Mitchell arrived at the cozy coffee shop, his heart racing with a mix of anticipation and nervousness. He spotted Mark Turner sitting at a corner table, engrossed in a book. Mark, a tall man in his mid-fifties, exuded an air of confidence and success. His salt-and-pepper hair added to his distinguished appearance.

As Eddie approached, Mark looked up, his eyes meeting Eddie's with a warm smile. "Eddie, it's great to see you," Mark greeted, extending his hand.

Eddie shook Mark's hand with a firm grip, returning the smile. "Likewise, Mark. Thanks for taking the time to meet with me."

Mark gestured toward an empty chair, inviting Eddie to sit. "No problem at all. I've heard you have taken a new role as an assistant softball coach. I'm always happy to help fellow coaches and leaders."

As they settled in, Eddie couldn't help but feel a sense of awe at Mark's accomplishments. Mark had not only coached high school lacrosse to multiple championships but also successfully ran his own business as its CEO. It was a combination of leadership roles Eddie found intriguing and inspiring.

"Mark, I have to say, your background in high school lacrosse coaching and your success as a business CEO are both impressive," Eddie began.

Mark chuckled modestly. "Thank you, Eddie. I've been fortunate to have had some great opportunities in my life. Coaching lacrosse and leading a company have taught me a lot about leadership, and there are certainly some parallels between the two."

Eddie leaned forward, eager to delve into the conversation. "I've been coaching my daughter's softball team, and I've realized that I have a lot to learn about effective coaching and leadership. I've also been facing similar challenges in my role as a sales leader, motivating and leading my team."

Mark nodded in understanding. "Coaching and leading in the corporate world have many similarities. It's all about inspiring people to work together toward a common goal, whether it's winning a game or achieving business objectives."

Eddie took a sip of his coffee, collecting his thoughts. "What I've observed, Mark, is that my attempts at motivating the softball team and my sales team haven't been as effective as I'd hoped. The girls on the softball team seem disengaged, and my sales team often lacks the drive to meet our targets."

Mark leaned back, considering Eddie's words. "Motivating and leading teams can be challenging, no doubt. It's about understanding what drives individuals, what makes them tick. You have to connect with them on a personal level, and genuinely care about their success. It's about them not you."

Eddie nodded, absorbing Mark's wisdom. "That makes sense. I believe that if I can become a better coach on the softball field, I can also become a better leader in my professional life. I'm here to learn, Mark, to understand what it takes to be an effective leader in both arenas."

Mark smiled, appreciating Eddie's sincerity. "Eddie, I'm here to help you on that journey. Let's start by discussing some key leadership principles that have served me well both in coaching and in business. We'll work together to adapt them to your coaching and leadership style."

As their conversation deepened, Eddie realized he was embarking on a transformative learning experience. The wisdom and guidance he would receive from Mark Turner held the promise of not only improving his coaching skills on the softball field but also his leadership abilities in the corporate world. This meeting marked the beginning of a remarkable journey that would challenge and inspire Eddie in ways he could never have imagined.

CHAPTER 5

Awakening Leadership

*"Before you are a leader, success is all about growing
yourself. When you become a leader, success is all about
growing others."*

—Jack Welch

As the aroma of freshly brewed coffee filled the air, their
meeting had transitioned from pleasantries to a deep dive
into the heart of leadership, and Eddie was eager to absorb
every bit of insight Mark had to offer.

"Leadership," Mark began, his voice carrying the weight
of experience, "is about creating a vision and empowers
others to achieve more than they thought possible. It's about
setting a clear and compelling direction that inspires people
to follow the leader's vision. Whether it's on the lacrosse
field or in the boardroom, a well-defined vision acts as our
North Star—it provides guidance and purpose."

Eddie leaned in, captivated by Mark's words. "That
makes a lot of sense. So how do you go about creating a
vision that truly resonates with your team?"

Mark began, "A story from my coaching days that underscores the importance of a leader's ability to envision the future for their team begins at the start of my second year of coaching. The entire team was made up of football players who were required by their state champion football coach to play lacrosse for conditioning for the next football season. The players were competitive athletes yet considered themselves football players and not lacrosse players. They needed a vision for the season, something to aspire to beyond staying in shape for football.

"As I looked at my players, I sensed their anticipation and hunger for competition. I knew that to inspire them and lead them to greatness, I needed to ignite their passion for lacrosse with a vision that would guide us through the trials and triumphs ahead."

So Mark began, "At the first practice I helped them envision what was possible by stating, 'Imagine standing on a sunny afternoon on that lacrosse field. The roar of the crowd is deafening, and the state championship trophy is within our grasp. It's the culmination of our hard work, the pinnacle of our journey together. That's our destination, and we will reach it.'

"As I spoke, I could see their faces light up with excitement, their eyes filled with determination. It wasn't enough for them to simply hear my words; they needed to visualize the scene and feel the exhilaration of becoming champions beyond the football field and deep in their hearts."

Mark paused for a moment, "Remember, a vision without a plan is just a dream. A vision alone is just the beginning; to make our dreams a reality, we needed a well-crafted strategy. The strategy I laid out for the lacrosse team at that moment consisted of:

"Skill development: We identified our weaknesses and devised a comprehensive plan to improve our skills. Every practice session was carefully designed to enhance our passing accuracy, defensive prowess, and overall teamwork.

"Team bonding: I believe that unity is the foundation of success. We organized team-building activities that transformed us from mere teammates into a tight-knit family, ready to support one another through every challenge.

"Game plans: To outmatch our opponents, we needed meticulous game plans. We scrutinized our adversaries, focusing on exploiting their vulnerabilities while maximizing our strengths. Every player knew their role inside and out.

"Mental resilience: I emphasized the importance of a strong mindset. I taught my players techniques to stay focused, handle pressure, and maintain unwavering confidence, even in the most high-stakes situations.

"Continuous growth: I fostered a growth mindset among my players. We saw setbacks as opportunities for growth. Constructive feedback was the key to their evolution, helping them reach their full potential."

Mark continued, "Eddie, this story illustrates the incredible impact of a leader's ability to envision the future for their team. It showcases how a compelling vision, when paired with a well-executed plan and a team's unwavering commitment, can lead to remarkable success."

Mark's eyes sparkled with enthusiasm as he delved deeper into the next critical topic of a player-first approach. "First and foremost, leadership must be people-focused. In my lacrosse coaching, I make it a point to understand each player's individual goals and aspirations. Some dream of playing at the collegiate level, while others are driven by the pure love of the game. In the business world, it's about helping your team members envision a clear career path and providing opportunities for their personal development."

Mark offered an affirming smile. "Eddie, it's a player-first approach in business as well. Your followers or team members' interests must be put before your own personal interests. It involves putting their needs and goals at the forefront of your mind. When people see that you're genuinely invested in their success, they become more committed to achieving the shared vision."

Eddie, scribbling notes in his ever-present notebook, was eager to internalize these principles. "Tell me more, what else is critically important?"

Mark paused for a moment, reflecting on the significance of emotional intelligence in leadership. "Emotional intelligence is a linchpin in both coaching and leadership. It's about understanding your own emotions and those of the individuals you're leading. In lacrosse, I've encountered players who needed an extra dose of encouragement, while others required a firm but fair hand. It's about adapting your leadership style to suit each situation and individual."

Eddie contemplated the idea of emotional intelligence. "I can see how that would help me connect with my softball team and my sales team on a much deeper level."

Mark nodded in agreement. "Absolutely, Eddie. The key is to be empathetic, to actively listen, and to genuinely care about the well-being of your team members. That's what fosters trust and loyalty."

As their conversation continued to flow, Mark shared captivating stories from his experiences in coaching lacrosse and leading a prosperous company. It was through these stories that these principles truly came to life.

One story centered on a lacrosse player named Ryan who struggled with self-doubt. Mark vividly recalled how he had taken the time to sit down with Ryan, understand his fears and insecurities, and help him see his potential. With Mark's guidance, Ryan transformed into a confident and skilled player, eventually earning a scholarship to play at the collegiate level.

"Eddie," Mark emphasized, "this was about creating a vision for Ryan—helping him see a future where he could excel. It was also about being people-focused, understanding his fears, and using emotional intelligence to provide the support he needed."

Another tale revolved around a pivotal moment in Mark's career as a CEO. He had faced a crisis in his company, and it was his ability to maintain a calm and composed demeanor, to inspire confidence in his team, and to adapt swiftly to the changing circumstances that had ultimately saved the day.

"Eddie," Mark continued, "leadership isn't just about leading in good times; it's about guiding your team through the storms as well. In that moment, I had to create a vision of a successful outcome, be intensely people-focused to keep my team motivated, and rely on emotional intelligence to navigate the uncertainty."

Eddie found himself hanging on every word, the stories resonating deeply with him. These narratives were not only about leadership but also about the human connection—the art of understanding, motivating, and empowering others.

Eddie couldn't help but feel a sense of inspiration welling up inside him as he listened to Mark's words. It was as if he had stumbled upon the missing pieces of the leadership puzzle that had eluded him for so long. He knew integrating these principles into his coaching on the softball field and his leadership in the corporate world would be transformative.

Mark concluded their conversation with a reassuring smile. "Eddie, remember that leadership is a journey, not a destination. It's about continuous growth and improvement. As you apply these principles to both coaching and your role as a sales leader, you'll witness positive changes in your teams."

Eddie left the coffee shop that day with a renewed sense of purpose burning within him. He had not only found a mentor in Mark Turner but also a guide on his path to becoming a more effective leader. The lessons about creating a vision, being people-focused, by helping others to envision what is possible for them, creating a development plan for their success, and practicing emotional intelligence would serve as the bedrock for his transformation.

Little did Eddie know the knowledge he had gleaned from Mark would not only revolutionize his coaching on the softball field but also usher in profound changes in his professional life. The journey was just beginning, and Eddie was fully prepared to embrace the challenges and opportunities lying ahead.

CHAPTER 6

Diamond Coaching Insights

"When one teaches, two learn."

—Robert Heinlein

Eddie's heart raced with anticipation as he drove to the softball field for practice. The conversation he had with Mark Turner had left an indelible mark on him. He knew the insights he had gained were not only going to transform their coaching but had the potential to change the lives of their players. As he arrived at the field, he couldn't wait to share his newfound knowledge with Lisa.

Lisa, who was setting up practice drills before the team arrived, noticed Eddie's enthusiastic stride. She waved at him, and he made his way over to her, a smile stretching across his face.

"Eddie, you look like you've discovered a hidden treasure. What's got you so fired up today?" Lisa asked, genuinely curious.

Eddie took a deep breath, his excitement barely contained. "Lisa, you won't believe the conversation I had yesterday with Mark Turner. He's an extraordinary guy. I can see how he won so many lacrosse championships and leads a successful company. We talked about coaching and leadership, and I can't wait to share what I learned with you."

Intrigued, yet hesitant, Lisa took a seat on the nearby bench, her attention focused on Eddie. "Coaching and leadership insights? I have been coaching for a while. I think I have probably heard it all at this point, but you seem excited, so let's hear it."

Eddie launched into a passionate retelling of the key principles Mark had emphasized. "First, creating a vision. Mark stressed that a clear and inspiring vision is crucial for our team. It's not just about winning games but about helping our players see their potential and the value of teamwork. What if we create a vision board together, something visual that reminds the team of our goals and aspirations?"

Lisa nodded. "I have seen that done before. It's effective and it will give the players a tangible reminder of what we're working towards."

Eddie's enthusiasm was infectious as he continued. "Next, Mark talked about being people-focused. It's about understanding each player's unique needs and motivations. Remember how we used to treat every player the same during practice drills? What if we tailor our coaching approach to each player's specific goals and positions they want to play? It might mean spending some extra one-on-one time with certain players."

Lisa considered their past coaching methods and realized the room for improvement. "You're probably right, Eddie. We have been coaching the team as one team and not focusing on the individual. If I step back, this might make sense. Some players need more attention in specific areas. Personalizing our coaching could make a significant difference, and the players will be more focused if it is a position they want to play. Let's give it a go."

Eddie was on a roll. "Lastly, Lisa, Mark emphasized the importance of emotional intelligence. We've sometimes been too tough on the players, pushing them hard without considering their emotional well-being. What if we actively listen to their concerns, empathize with their struggles, and provide constructive feedback in a more supportive way? It's about building trust and a positive team atmosphere."

Lisa nodded in agreement. "I can see how that would help the players feel more comfortable and motivated to improve."

As practice continued, Eddie and Lisa put these newfound insights into action, focusing on different players for each key area from Eddie's conversation with Mark.

CHAPTER 7

Between the Bat and Empathy

"Great leaders are willing to sacrifice the numbers to save the people. Poor leaders sacrifice the people to save the numbers."

—Simon Sinek

The next day, Eddie found himself back in the corporate world with the pressure of slowing sales and a dire need to turn around his sales team. In the hushed ambience of his monthly team meeting, frustration and concern showed on Eddie's forehead. Sales success seemed elusive as his team followed the path of bare-minimum prospecting, reacting passively with clients, and an unfortunate few casting shadows of negativity on their peers. Eddie, on the verge of expressing his exasperation, paused—reflecting on the profound lessons of emotional intelligence bestowed upon him by Mark and a haunting experience from the not-so-distant past.

A year earlier, the walls of Aerospace Technologies witnessed a climactic meeting, orchestrated by the assertive yet volatile president, Mike. Aerospace Technologies struggled to achieve their sales targets and were not able to meet technology implementation deadlines for their clients, which impacted their ability to retain their top clients. The atmosphere before the meeting was charged with trepidation as Eddie, alongside Jane, the head of marketing, and Rich, the head of customer service, entered the room where the rest of the senior leaders, each carrying the weight of their respective domains, convened. Mike, notorious for his aggressive leadership, had summoned them to dissect the organization's failure to meet sales targets and technology implementation deadlines. No one was excited about this meeting, full well knowing what might lie in store for the team. However, to everyone's surprise, Mike was not there yet.

At the front of the room was a flip chart with the words: "Are You Delivering?" As everyone found their seats and read the flip chart, Mike walked in brandishing a baseball bat. As much as Eddie fondly remembered playing baseball and now coaching softball, he did not have a good feeling about this situation. Mike slowly walked to the front the room, visibly upset, red faced, and confronted the leaders with an accusatory fervor, "Do you all know where we are on our goal? DO YOU? I ask you ARE YOU DELIVERING???" As Mike yelled, the emotional turbulence escalated as the bat met the flip chart, shattering the illusion of composure. "The answer is NO! You are not delivering!"

The air in the room seemed to disappear; everyone held their breath, nervous to say a word or even move. Mike stood at the front of the room and slammed the bat down on the table. "Now, we need to hit our goals for the business; you are the leaders of the company, and we need answers!"

Mike went on, "Bob, you lead technology implementation across the organization for our clients; what is the delay!?!" Bob, a genius in the technology world, was also an introvert. He had great respect from his team for his passion for technology, the caring he had for each member of his team, and his ability to solve problems.

Bob nervously spoke, "Andy, my lead tech specialist, has been working on the implementation issue for a few weeks now, and—"

Mike interrupted, "A few weeks now, this should be fixed by now. . . ." Everyone could see the anger in Mike's face as he raised his voice and said, "I want Andy gone by the end of the day!"

Reflecting on that episode, Eddie contemplated the stark contrast between Mike's tyrannical approach and the principles of emotional intelligence shared by Mark Turner. The indelible scars left by that meeting underscored the repercussions of a leader lacking empathy, self-regulation, and the ability to inspire collaboration. Eddie could barely remember all the specifics from the meeting, although he did recall that not one senior leader in that room was willing to offer an idea or share a suggestion on how to improve the overall business outcomes. To this day, leaders still talk about how they felt at that meeting, unwilling to share insights, partner together, and a loss of credibility in Mike as a leader. Over the months following the meeting, a few of the senior leaders on Mike's team left the company, including Bob, who was severely impacted by Mike's outburst toward him and his team at the meeting.

Now, at the precipice of his own team meeting, Eddie embraced the concept shared by Mark Turner on emotional intelligence. He recognized the power of self-awareness, understanding the ripples of his own emotions and their potential impact. Rather than succumbing to frustration, he chose a path of reflection, a conscious decision to lead with emotional intelligence.

As the meeting unfolded, Eddie shared his frustrations and concerns. "Team, I've sensed a collective struggle in our approach and results. Let's consider this as an opportunity to realign our efforts." His words, measured and empathetic, set the tone for a different narrative—one where challenges would be addressed collaboratively. Eddie showcased emotional self-management by steering the challenges away from blame, fostering an environment where every team member felt heard.

Seeking to understand before being understood, Eddie turned the spotlight on individual team members. "Each of you plays a crucial role in our success. Jennifer and Dave, you mentioned challenges you are both facing in prospecting. Who has experienced this struggle in the past and can share ideas and strategies in overcoming this obstacle?"

After an in-depth idea share amongst the team, Eddie shared the other struggles in the business and engaged the team for innovative and collaborative ideas to solve the problems. The empathy woven into Eddie's leadership fabric became apparent as he acknowledged the challenges faced by individual team members. Eddie was an embodiment of emotional intelligence that stood in stark contrast to the bat-wielding theatrics of Mike.

The room transformed into one of collaboration. Eddie leveraged his social skills to facilitate the exchange of ideas. Empathy, a key principle of emotional intelligence, echoed through Eddie's words as he sought to understand his team's perspective while he inspired the team with a shared vision, aligning individual efforts toward collective success.

As Eddie navigated the complexities of the meeting, the themes of emotional intelligence shared by Mark resonated, bringing his team forward to one where frustrations were acknowledged, challenges were met with empathy, and solutions were crafted through collective partnership.

CHAPTER 8

Purpose-Driven Softball

*"If my mind can conceive it, and my heart can believe it—
then I can achieve it."*

—Muhammad Ali

After seeing the impact of Mark's recommendations with his sales team, Eddie was invigorated to get back with the softball team. Eddie and Lisa planned on implementing Mark's suggestions as soon as possible. At the start of the next practice, they called the team together for a team meeting. With the departure of the head coach and assistant coach early in the season, Lisa becoming the new head coach and Eddie joining the coaching staff, both Lisa and Eddie had faced skepticism from some of the players and, of course, a few of the parents. After all, Lisa was new to the head coach position and Eddie was new to coaching this group of girls, while the team had grown accustomed to its previous coaches and their style.

As they stood before the expectant faces of their players on that bright spring morning, Eddie and Lisa could feel a shift in the atmosphere. They had earned the respect and admiration of the team over the last few weeks through hard work, dedication, and a genuine passion for the game. The players had begun to see their coaches were invested in their growth and success.

Eddie, his voice filled with conviction, began, "Girls, we are going to be on this journey together, and we will face our fair share of challenges. I know that some of you had doubts when I first stepped onto this field as assistant coach."

Riley, the star first baseman and Eddie's daughter, glanced around at her teammates, noting the nods of agreement. Even she had been one of the players who had questioned if her father would be a good coach, even though she was happy he was spending more time with her and her team.

Lisa continued, "But today, we stand here united, coaches and players. Eddie and I want to share a common purpose and vision for the team:

"The relentless pursuit of excellence: The Blue Lightning shapes student-athletes who are successful academically and athletically and who are prepared for success on the field, at home, and in the community. High expectations, integrity, a relentless attention to the fundamentals, and work ethic are hallmarks of the Blue Lightning.

"We want to continually improve, not just for ourselves but for each other. We believe in this team, and we believe in all of you."

Molly, the catcher, exchanged a knowing look with Ellie, the shortstop. They had seen Eddie and Lisa's commitment to improving the team, from refining their strategies to spending countless hours on individual coaching sessions.

Eddie took a step closer to the players, his eyes reflecting the determination within him. "Our vision is to become champions, to be the best team out there. It's not just about winning games; it's about becoming the best versions of ourselves as athletes and individuals. Our victories are not measured only in runs scored or games won; they are also in the friendships we build, the lessons we learn, and the character we develop."

Lily, the second baseman, whispered to Hannah, the centerfielder, "They really mean it, don't they? They want us to succeed."

Lisa added, "To achieve this vision, it'll take teamwork, discipline, and a belief in each other. We want you to know that we're here for you, not just as coaches but as mentors and supporters. Together, we can achieve anything."

Kennedy, the right fielder, who had initially been skeptical of the new coaching duo, nodded appreciatively. She whispered to Sophie, the third baseman, "I think they're onto something, Sophie. Maybe we can do this."

Eddie concluded, "So let's start today with purpose and determination. Let's work together, support each other, and give everything we've got. We believe in this team, and we know that together we can achieve greatness."

The players responded with a resounding cheer, their doubts replaced by a growing belief in their coaches and their vision. For the first time, they felt united with Eddie and Lisa, bound by a common purpose transcending wins and losses.

As they went into practice that day, there was a newfound energy on the field. The players ran drills with enthusiasm, communicated seamlessly, and pushed each other to excel. They were no longer just a group of individuals; they were a team with a shared vision, ready to conquer the challenges that lay ahead.

As Eddie and Riley arrived home that evening after practice, there was a noticeable shift in Riley's demeanor. Instead of being absorbed in her cell phone like her typical teenage self, she seemed eager and animated. As the family sat down for dinner, Riley's eyes sparkled with excitement as she glanced first at her mom, Erin, and then turned to her dad, her smile widening.

"Dad, I've been thinking," Riley began, her voice filled with enthusiasm, "it's been amazing having you coach softball with us. Today's practice, when you talked about having a vision for the team, it really got me thinking."

Eddie's eyes filled with pride at his daughter's words. "Thanks, sweetheart. I'm grateful to be part of the team and to share these moments with you."

Riley nodded eagerly, her excitement evident. "Mom, Dad's words about vision and purpose today made me realize there is more than just softball. I think we should have a vision for our family too."

Erin leaned in closer, intrigued by Riley's suggestion. "What do you mean, Riley?"

Riley's smile widened as she explained, "Well, like Dad said, it's about having a common goal and working together towards it. I think if we sit down as a family and talk about our dreams and goals, we can come up with our own vision for the future."

Eddie's eyes lit up with excitement, nodding in agreement. "I love that idea, Riley. It's crucial for us to support each other and have a clear direction for where we're headed as a family."

Erin, fully aware how softball was bringing their family closer together, reached out to squeeze Riley's hand, her heart filled with warmth. "I couldn't agree more, sweetheart. Let's make it happen."

As they continued their dinner, the conversation flowed effortlessly, each member of the family sharing their hopes and aspirations for the future. In that moment, surrounded by love and support, they knew that together they could achieve anything. And with their shared vision guiding them, the journey ahead seemed brighter and more promising than ever before.

In the midst of their discussion, Eddie and Erin exchanged a look of appreciation for the transformative impact this journey, both in softball and as a family, was having on Riley and on their family as a whole. It was a profound realization, marking a significant shift from where they had been only a few short weeks ago.

CHAPTER 9

Visionary Sales Strategies

"To grasp and hold a vision, that is the very essence of successful leadership."

—Ronald Reagan

Eddie was well aware leading a sales team wasn't just about quotas and targets—it was about inspiring individuals to work cohesively toward a shared purpose. Mark Turner's insights into creating a vision had made an impact on the softball field and was transforming his family, and he was eager to implement these lessons in his role as a sales manager.

Shortly after setting a vision for the softball team, Eddie gathered his sales team for a meeting. They were a diverse group, each with their unique strengths and aspirations. Eddie knew a compelling vision could be the driving force uniting them and building a path for success following their last meeting.

"Team," Eddie began, "I've been doing some research on what makes high-performing sales teams truly exceptional. One key element that stands out is having a vision that inspires and motivates us. I believe it's time for us to create our own vision—one that guides our efforts, fuels our passion, and sets us apart."

Curiosity filled the room as his team leaned in to listen.

Eddie continued, "Our vision will be more than just a statement; it will be a source of inspiration and a driving force for us. It will shape the way we work, the decisions we make, and the impact we have on our clients."

A vision statement can be a vital part of an organization and the strategic planning process. With Mark's guidance, Eddie followed the key steps in facilitating an engaging session for the entire team to work together and align on a shared vision. The steps he took with the team allowed them to create an inspirational vision for the future.

Steps in creating a vision:

Dream Big, But Stay Grounded: A vision statement should be ambitious and bold, but remember, it should also be realistic. It should reflect what your organization genuinely aspires to achieve.

Be Clear and Concise: The best vision statements are clear, concise, and easily understood. They avoid jargon and complex language.

Make it Inspirational: Your vision statement should inspire your team and stakeholders. It should convey passion and commitment.

Reflect Your Organization's Core Values: The vision statement should align with the core values of your organization. It should reflect what you stand for and believe in.

Involve Your Team: Get input from your team during the vision statement writing process. This promotes buy-in and ensures the vision reflects the aspirations of the entire organization.

After a day of working together on their vision, the team was closer as individuals, knowing they each participated and added their perspective on building a vision for the future. As everyone returned from a well-needed break, Eddie read aloud their final vision statement.

Our Vision for Excellence:

"Elevating Aerospace Safety: Our Vision is to
Pioneer Innovative Solutions and Set the
Standard for Unparalleled Safety in the Skies.
We Envision a Future Where Every Flight
Inspires Confidence and Every Journey is
Secured with Cutting-Edge Technology and a
Commitment to Excellence."

Eddie paused, allowing the vision to resonate with his team. He noticed a spark of enthusiasm in their eyes. They were not just hearing words; they were envisioning a future where they played a vital role.

One of his sales representatives, Jennifer, spoke up. "Eddie, this vision is more than just a goal—it's a purpose. It's about making a real impact on our clients and being the best at what we do. I'm excited to be a part of this."

Others chimed in, expressing their commitment to the vision and their eagerness to contribute. It was evident the session to create a vision had struck a chord within the team.

As days turned into weeks, the team fully embraced the vision. Their approach to work shifted from merely meeting targets to genuinely caring about their clients' success. Collaborative efforts flourished, and they found motivation in the pursuit of excellence.

The results were impressive. Their performance skyrocketed, but more importantly, their sense of fulfillment and purpose grew stronger every day.

Eddie had learned from his conversations with Mark that a compelling vision could turn a group of individuals into a cohesive, purpose-driven team. He realized the power of a well-crafted vision extended far beyond the softball field—it could transform the landscape of the sales world, and he was ready to lead the way.

CHAPTER 10

SMART Goals

"Hope is not a strategy."

—Vince Lombardi

The next week, Eddie brought his team back together in the conference room overlooking the city's skyline, eager to outline a strategic approach that would not only drive revenue but redefine their aerospace technology company's success in the market.

Eddie, leaning confidently against the oval conference room table, began, "Team, success is a journey, and to embark on this journey, we need a roadmap—a sales strategy that not only meets our objectives but propels us to new heights to achieve the vision we built together last week."

Eddie began to share the three-pronged approach to the sales strategy:

Customer-Centric Approach: "Our journey to success begins with our customers," Eddie stated emphatically. "We'll adopt a customer-centric approach, understanding their needs, pain points, and aspirations. Our solutions won't just meet specifications; they'll exceed expectations."

Strategic Partnerships: "Success is not a solo flight," Eddie emphasized. "We'll forge strategic partnerships with key players in the industry. These collaborations will not only enhance our product capabilities but also open new avenues for growth."

Market Expansion and Penetration: "Our sales strategy involves both depth and breadth," Eddie explained. "We'll penetrate existing markets with intensified sales efforts while simultaneously exploring untapped regions. This dual-focused approach will maximize our market presence. This ensures our portfolio caters to the broad spectrum of the industry, allowing us to aim towards our vision of inspiring confidence in every flight across all airlines, commercial and private."

As the sales team absorbed the strategic plan, a sense of excitement filled the room. The sales strategy wasn't just a roadmap; it was a dynamic plan designed to navigate the complex landscape of the aerospace market.

Eddie continued, with more specific direction on expectations and goals for the team. Mark had shared the valuable process of developing SMART goals and Eddie wanted to implement this concept into his team to assist in clarity of expectations and direction.

In the heart of a strategic workshop, Eddie gathered his team for a profound journey into the world of SMART goals. With an easel and markers at his disposal, he began illustrating each facet, making the abstract tangible. Eddie, with a gleam of excitement in his eyes, had something transformative to share on SMART goals.

"Team," Eddie began, "we've been soaring high with our vision and strategy, but now it's time to chart a course that ensures we not only reach our destination but do so with precision and purpose."

Curiosity painted the faces of his team as Eddie unveiled the concept of SMART goals.

"Let's imagine this," Eddie started, sketching a target on the flipchart. "Our objectives are like this bullseye. To hit it, we need specificity. That's the *S* in SMART."

Transitioning to the *M* for measurable, Eddie continued, "Now, let's not stop at vague aspirations. We need to measure our progress. Imagine you're on a road trip, and you want to know how far you've come. That's the essence of being measurable. Achievable," Eddie said with conviction, "is about turning dreams into reality."

As Eddie delved into relevant, he connected their goals with the bigger picture. "Every goal we set should resonate with our broader objectives." Finally, Eddie circled time-bound.

"Time is our most valuable resource. To give our goals the urgency they need, we're setting timelines. Picture this as a countdown, ticking toward our success. Our goals are not open-ended; they are bound by time."

To bring this concept to life, Eddie invited his team on an airborne journey into an example of SMART goals. As they gathered around, he began weaving an analogy that soared through the skies and connected to their business.

SMART Goals

S—PECIFIC

M—EASURABLE

A—CHIEVABLE

R—ELEVANT

T—IME BOUND

1. Specific:

Eddie projected an image of an airport departure board with a single destination: Success City. "Imagine we're on a flight. Our destination is clear—Success City. It's not enough to say 'Let's take off.' We need a specific flight plan, detailing our route to that city."

2. Measurable:

A cockpit dashboard appeared on the screen. "This is our dashboard. Every gauge tells us something measurable. Our altitude, speed, and fuel—they're tangible metrics. We need to know, at any point, how far we are from reaching our destination."

3. Achievable:

Eddie then introduced the concept of the aircraft itself. "Our plane represents our goals. If we set our goal as interstellar travel with our current technology, it's not achievable. But a flight to Success City? Absolutely. Our goals should stretch us, not break us."

4. Relevant:

A network of flight routes emerged on the screen. "Our journey is part of a larger air network. Each route is a goal, but they're all connected. Our specific goal should make sense in the context of our overall flight plan. If it's a detour, it's not relevant."

5. Time-Bound:

A flight schedule was displayed. "Time is of the essence in air travel. We have departure and arrival times. Our goals are similar. We're not flying aimlessly; we have a schedule. Setting a defined timeframe adds the urgency needed to reach our destination."

As Eddie's aviation analogy unfolded, the team envisioned their goals as waypoints in a flight plan. The departure board, cockpit dashboard, aircraft, flight network, and schedule were not just symbols; they were the elements of a strategic flight.

As Eddie concluded, the team sat in thoughtful silence, absorbing the impact of this new approach. SMART goals weren't just a set of directives; they were the compass guiding them through the intricacies of their collective journey. The room buzzed with a sense of clarity and purpose—a testament to the transformative power of strategic goal-setting. There was a newfound sense of purpose with an aligned vision for the team followed by a strategy and tactics that would allow the team to achieve their goals and objectives.

CHAPTER 11

Diamonds in the Sky

"Take those chances and you can achieve greatness, whereas if you go conservative, you'll never know."

—Danica Patrick

Amidst the blooming of flowers and the gentle sway of trees on a picturesque spring day, Maddie, the talented young pitcher, found herself with a heart full of dreams. She had always known she wanted to excel in softball ever since joining a team as a young girl, but the specifics of her future remained hazy.

One afternoon, as the sun bathed the softball field in a warm, golden glow, Maddie decided it was time to share her aspirations with Lisa and Eddie. She sat between them on the grass, the soft breeze ruffling her hair and a sense of urgency propelling her words.

"I love to play softball and want to keep playing after the season," Maddie began, her voice carrying the weight of her love of the game. "But I don't know where or how far I can go with this."

Eddie and Lisa exchanged knowing glances, recognizing their role in extending the passion and easing the uncertainty in Maddie's eyes. They understood this moment was a crossroads, a chance to help her unearth the depths of her dreams.

Eddie leaned in, his voice filled with encouragement. "Maddie, you are a great player with passion for the game. What can you imagine beyond just this season? Dreams have a way of expanding, of surprising us with their vastness. What can you imagine, the sky's the limit? What does that future look like to you?"

Maddie closed her eyes, allowing her imagination to roam freely. She saw herself not only as a remarkable athlete but also as a trailblazer, a motivator, and a beacon of hope. She envisioned a future where she used her journey to inspire others, a future where she could make a difference beyond the softball diamond.

As Maddie shared her hopes and dreams with Eddie and Lisa, they listened intently. Her dreams now stretched far beyond the confines of the softball field. She saw herself thriving at Duke University, not only as pitcher for their softball team but also as a student, a leader, and a symbol of perseverance.

Maddie's vision had developed because she had recently watched Duke's softball team's remarkable journey to the College World Series. It was during those intense games, as she watched the players exhibit resilience, teamwork, and unwavering determination, that she had realized where she wanted to be.

Eddie and Lisa, fueled by Maddie's newfound aspirations, promised to stand by her side. They pledged to help her become not just an outstanding athlete but also a leader, a mentor, and a source of inspiration. They would support her in developing the skills, determination, and wisdom needed to navigate the path to her dreams. Eddie and Lisa began working with Maddie weekly on a specific development plan to accomplish her goal.

On that spring day, Maddie's love of the game evolved beyond the current season on the softball diamond. It became a vision of leadership, of impact, and of leaving an enduring legacy. The journey ahead would be filled with challenges, but now Maddie had a clear vision of the future and was no longer pursuing a dream; she was chasing a specific goal, a vision as boundless as the clear blue sky above.

CHAPTER 12

Career Visions

"A leader who producers other leaders multiples their influence."

—John Maxwell

As the spring season unfolded on the softball field, Eddie found himself immersed in another arena of leadership—his role at work as a sales leader. He had always been dedicated to his job, but the newfound insights he had gained through coaching had ignited a fresh passion within him.

One day, Eddie noticed a sense of restlessness in one of his sales representatives, Jennifer. She was undoubtedly talented, but there was a spark missing in her approach to her career. Eddie had been there himself, standing at a crossroads between proficiency and aspiration, and he felt a responsibility to guide her toward her own vision of her career.

During a one-on-one meeting, Eddie gently broached the subject. "Jennifer," he began, "I've seen your potential, and I believe you can achieve great things here. But I also sense that there might be something more you're yearning for. Have you ever thought about your long-term career path?"

Jennifer's brow furrowed as she pondered the question. It was clear she hadn't given it much consideration. "Honestly, Eddie, I'm not sure. I'm good at sales, and I enjoy it, but I don't know where it's taking me."

Eddie smiled warmly, his eyes reflecting a genuine desire to help her discover her path. "That's okay, Jennifer. Sometimes, we need to take a step back and think about what truly inspires us. Imagine yourself in five, ten, or twenty years. What do you want your career to look like? What legacy do you want to leave?"

Jennifer took a moment to envision her future. She began to paint a mental picture of herself as a seasoned sales professional not just achieving targets but also mentoring and guiding a team of her own. The thought filled her with a newfound sense of purpose.

Eddie saw the spark in Jennifer's eyes, just as he had seen the spark in Maddie's eyes on the softball field, and recognized the birth of a vision. He leaned forward, his voice carrying the weight of encouragement. "Jennifer, your journey doesn't have to be limited to sales quotas. You can become a leader, a mentor, someone who helps others reach their potential. Picture yourself in a role where you're not only excelling but also inspiring those around you."

Over the coming weeks and months, Eddie became a mentor to Jennifer, much as he had been to Maddie. He shared stories of his own career path, the challenges he had faced, and the mentors who had guided him. He encouraged her to attend workshops, take on leadership roles within the sales team, and envision her future with clarity.

Gradually, Jennifer's vision expanded. She began to see herself as a leader within the company, guiding and inspiring her colleagues to excel. Her sales performance improved, but more importantly, her sense of purpose grew exponentially. She was no longer just chasing sales targets; she was on a path to becoming a leader.

As Eddie watched Jennifer's transformation, he realized the principles of leadership he had learned through coaching softball were equally applicable in the corporate world. Whether on the softball field or in the boardroom, the essence of leadership lay in helping individuals discover their visions and empowering them to pursue those dreams with unwavering determination.

In Eddie and Jennifer's next meeting, Eddie continued the discussion on career planning and asked Jennifer to envision her retirement party. "Close your eyes, Jennifer, and picture it," he urged. "You're surrounded by colleagues and friends. You're cutting the cake at your retirement party. Tell me, what job are you retiring from?"

Jennifer's eyes remained closed for a moment, and then a smile spread across her face. "I'm retiring from the position of head of sales," she said, her voice filled with confidence.

Eddie nodded, a sense of pride swelling within him. "That's the vision, Jennifer. Let's work together to make it a reality."

And so their journey continued, fueled by Jennifer's vision and the support from Eddie, who believed in her potential. Eddie had not only transformed the softball team on the field but was now guiding a talented sales representative toward her dreams, proving the power of leadership knows no bounds.

CHAPTER 13

Beyond the Diamond

"If your actions inspire others to dream more, learn more, do more and become more, you are a leader."

—John Quincy Adams

Eddie and Lisa's commitment to cultivating leadership within their softball team went hand in hand with their dedication to putting the players first. They recognized each member of their girls' team had unique qualities and aspirations, and it was essential to tailor their coaching approach accordingly.

One sunny afternoon after practice, Eddie and Lisa gathered the players for a team meeting. They found a shaded spot near the field, where the girls could relax and engage in an open conversation. The coaches were keenly aware of the potential within each player and wanted to ensure they nurtured not just athletes but also confident and empowered young women.

As they sat down, Lisa began, "We've always believed that our team is more than just a softball team. It's a group of talented, strong, and determined young women. Each one of you has unique strengths, dreams, and ambitions, both on and off the field."

Eddie nodded in agreement, adding, "Our role as coaches isn't just about improving your softball skills. It's also about helping you become the best version of yourselves. We want to understand your goals, your challenges, and how we can support you in achieving them."

The girls looked at each other, pleasantly surprised by the coaches' approach. They had expected another practice-focused discussion, not a heartfelt conversation about their individual aspirations.

Over the following weeks, Eddie and Lisa continued to emphasize the importance of personal development alongside athletic growth. They encouraged the girls to set both short-term and long-term goals, whether related to softball, academics, or personal life. By doing so, they aimed to instill a sense of purpose and self-belief in each player.

The benefits of this player-focused approach soon became evident. Players felt more comfortable approaching Eddie and Lisa with their concerns, whether it was about a challenging math class, challenges on the field, or struggles with self-confidence. The coaches provided guidance, shared their own life experiences, and connected the players with resources to help them overcome obstacles.

As the season progressed, the girls' performance on the field began to reflect their personal growth. They played with a newfound confidence, not just in their softball skills but in themselves as individuals. It was clear that the coaches' investment in the players' personal development was paying off.

The player-focused approach was also transforming Eddie's relationship with his daughter, Riley. Eddie found himself astounded by the evolution in his relationship with her. No longer was there a distant connection as before the softball season began; now, a profound closeness permeated both their time on and off the field. Since Riley's suggestion of building a vision for the family together, she had developed her own goals. Riley's aspirations soared beyond mere proficiency on the softball field; she harbored a distinct ambition—to clinch victory in the home run derby at the season's end. With Eddie's guidance and support, Riley committed herself to perfecting her hitting skills, dedicating extra hours in the batting cage to meticulously refine her technique. Eddie, fueled by his daughter's fervor and dedication, stood by her side, offering tailored coaching and drills to amplify her power and precision.

The beauty of the player-focused approach extended beyond Eddie's relationship with Riley. The girls on the team developed a strong bond, supporting each other's dreams and celebrating each other's successes. It wasn't just about winning games; it was about nurturing a sense of camaraderie, resilience, and empowerment.

One evening, as the sun dipped below the horizon after a particularly productive practice, Lisa turned to Eddie and said, "Our team is flourishing, Eddie. It's not just about their skills; it's about the young women they're becoming. I couldn't be prouder."

Eddie smiled, fully aware of the impact of their player-focused coaching. "When you put the players first, when you invest in their dreams and their growth, it's amazing to see how they can exceed even their own expectations."

The journey of their softball team was a testament to the benefits of prioritizing the players' well-being and personal development. It was a reminder that by focusing on the individuals within the team, they could create better athletes and confident young women.

CHAPTER 14

Leadership Lessons

"You can measure a man's character by the choices he makes under pressure."

—Winston Churchill

Eddie had put into practice the leadership insights he had gained from his previous meetings with Mark Turner. The results were undeniable. The softball team had blossomed into a tight-knit group of motivated athletes, and Eddie's sales team at work had experienced a surge in productivity. However, Eddie was well aware leadership was an ever-evolving journey, and he thirsted for more wisdom.

So on a crisp, sunny, Saturday morning, Eddie met Mark at the coffee shop that had become their preferred meeting spot. As they savored their steaming cups of coffee, Eddie couldn't help but express his profound appreciation. "Mark, I can't thank you enough for the guidance you've given me. The positive changes I've witnessed in both my coaching and my sales team are remarkable. Morale is soaring, and I feel like I'm finally making a real impact."

Mark smiled warmly, acknowledging Eddie's growth. "Eddie, it's gratifying to see how you've taken the principles to heart and made them your own. Leadership is an ongoing journey, and there's always room to grow."

Mark added, "Understanding your own strengths and limitations as a leader is at the core of effective leadership. It's about recognizing what you excel at and where you may need support. When you're aware of your strengths, you can leverage them to inspire and guide your team. At the same time, acknowledging your limitations allows you to seek help or delegate tasks where others might excel."

Eddie reflected on his journey so far. "I've learned that it's okay not to have all the answers. I've started to delegate tasks that aren't in my wheelhouse and empower team members who have strengths where I don't."

Mark continued, "Approachability is another essential characteristic. Your team, whether on the softball field or in the board room, should feel comfortable coming to you with their concerns, ideas, or even mistakes. When you're approachable, you create an environment of open communication and trust."

Eddie nodded, recalling instances when he had encouraged his players and sales team to share their thoughts openly. "Approachability fosters collaboration and innovation," he added.

"Next, let's talk about inspiring your team," Mark said. "As a leader, you have the power to motivate and energize your team. Share your vision with enthusiasm, lead by example, and remind them of their importance in achieving the collective goal."

Eddie remembered the moment when he and Lisa had shared their grand vision with the softball team. "Inspiring others is about connecting them to a shared purpose. It's powerful."

Mark leaned forward, his eyes reflecting a depth of experience. "Eddie, let me share some examples from my journey where these leadership characteristics and a few other key characteristics played a pivotal role."

Understanding Strengths and Limitations:

"In my early days of coaching lacrosse," Mark began, "I had a star player and team captain, named Daniel, who was incredibly talented but had a tendency to be overly competitive. His drive often led to clashes with his teammates. I recognized his strengths on the field but also saw the strain it put on team dynamics."

Mark explained how he had a candid conversation with Daniel about channeling his competitive spirit into leadership. "I helped him see that by using his drive to inspire and support his teammates, he could become a role model. Daniel eventually embraced this idea, and it transformed his relationship with the team. Understanding his strengths and limitations was key to this transformation."

Approachability:

Mark continued, "In my role as a CEO, approachability is crucial. One day, an employee on our production line approached me with an innovative idea for streamlining our operations. I could have dismissed it, but I chose to listen attentively. That idea turned out to be a game-changer for our company, leading to increased efficiency and profits."

Mark emphasized fostering an environment where employees felt comfortable approaching him with ideas had led to numerous innovations within the company. "Being approachable isn't just about being open to feedback; it's about actively seeking it."

Inspiration:

Mark's eyes gleamed as he recounted a lacrosse season where his team faced adversity. "We were down by three goals in the final quarter of a championship game. The players were disheartened, but I gathered them and shared a vision of a triumphant comeback. I reminded them of their months of hard work and how it had brought them to this moment."

The team rallied, drawing inspiration from Mark's words. With each possession the team pushed forward relentlessly, refusing to let up on the offensive pressure. Their defense shut down the opponent's offense setting the stage for victory. They went on to win the game by one, creating a cherished memory of teamwork and resilience. "Leadership is about igniting the fire within your team, especially during challenging times," Mark emphasized.

Integrity:

"As a CEO, maintaining integrity in every aspect of business is nonnegotiable," Mark stated firmly. He recounted a time when the company faced a choice that could have resulted in short-term gains but compromised their long-term reputation. Mark chose the path of integrity, even though it meant taking a financial hit.

"Ultimately, our commitment to integrity strengthened our relationships with clients, employees, and partners. It's a testament to the enduring value of doing the right thing, no matter the immediate cost."

Authenticity:

Mark shared a personal story from his lacrosse coaching days. "One season, I was dealing with my own challenges outside of coaching. Instead of hiding it, I shared my struggles with the team. I was vulnerable, and I let them see the real me."

The team responded with empathy and support, and our bond grew stronger. "Authenticity builds trust, and trust is the foundation of effective leadership," Mark affirmed.

Work Ethic:

Mark shared a pivotal moment while leading his company. "During a period of rapid growth, our company faced immense pressure to meet deadlines. I rolled up my sleeves alongside my team on the production floor, working late nights and weekends to ensure we met our commitments."

He explained his willingness to put in the hard work inspired his employees to do the same. "Leaders must lead by example. A strong work ethic is contagious."

As Mark concluded his stories, Eddie couldn't help but be inspired. These real-life examples brought the principles of leadership to life. He realized leadership wasn't a theoretical concept but a practical, everyday commitment to understanding, inspiring, and empowering others. Eddie left the coffee shop with a newfound appreciation for the power of leadership in action and a deep sense of gratitude for his mentor, Mark.

CHAPTER 15

Strengths and Limitations

"Knowing your weakness, is a strength."
—Dr. Toylin Omofoye

Eddie walked back from the coffee shop with a sense of fulfillment. Mark had shared invaluable insights about leadership, and Eddie was eager to put them into practice, especially the idea of understanding strengths and limitations. He knew he had to share these lessons with Lisa and, more importantly, apply them to their coaching journey.

Prepared to delve into the insights Mark shared about leadership, Eddie asked Lisa to meet an hour before practice to discuss. Eddie was waiting when Lisa arrived. She was curious about Eddie's expression. "You seem invigorated. What did Mark have to say?"

Eddie settled down next to Lisa in the dugout, eager to share his newfound wisdom. "Mark emphasized the importance of understanding our strengths and limitations, both as leaders and as coaches. I think this could continue to evolve our coaching to the next level."

Lisa nodded, her interest piqued. "Go on, Eddie."

Eddie began by pointing out their strengths as coaches. "Take you, for example, Lisa. Your ability to connect with the players on a personal level is extraordinary. You understand their concerns and aspirations, and that builds trust and loyalty."

Lisa smiled, appreciating the recognition. "And you, Eddie, have an incredible knack for strategizing and adapting. Your analytical thinking and ability to come up with innovative practice drills are invaluable to the team."

"But it's equally important to recognize our limitations," Eddie said thoughtfully. "We have to admit that we both struggle with time management. Our full-time jobs and family commitments often leave us stretched thin. Committing to coach for the season has been a blessing with my ability to deepen my relationship with Riley and has given me purpose that has ultimately strengthened our family bond. However, one consistent challenge has been time management when everything is a priority."

Lisa added, "And sometimes, we may get too emotionally invested in the game. It can cloud our judgment and affect our decision-making during critical moments."

Eddie and Lisa realized understanding their strengths and limitations could be a game-changer in their coaching approach. They decided to leverage each other's strengths more effectively. Lisa would focus on connecting with the players, building their confidence, and fostering team spirit.

Eddie would take the lead in designing practice sessions, strategies, and game plans.

They also acknowledged the need to address their time-management issues. They would set more realistic expectations for themselves and thoughtfully prioritize the most important aspects of the practice and game planning.

As the weeks passed, the impact of this approach became evident. Lisa's rapport with the players deepened, and they began to confide in her even more. Eddie's innovative practice sessions challenged and improved the team's skills.

Their recognition of their limitations allowed them to manage their time better. They started to arrive at practices and games well-prepared and with a clearer focus.

The team, as a whole, seemed more motivated and united as they saw their players working together seamlessly, each focusing on what they did best. Eddie and Lisa's ability to share their limitations with the team made them more relatable to the players, and it fostered a supportive and collaborative environment.

Eddie and Lisa couldn't help but feel a sense of pride as they watched their players grow and flourish. The lessons they had learned from Mark transformed not only their coaching style but also the dynamics of their softball team.

In their journey to become better leaders and coaches, Eddie and Lisa were discovering the importance of understanding their strengths and recognizing their limitations was the key to unlocking their full potential as coaches and leaders.

CHAPTER 16

Struggles to Triumph

"We all have a tendency to avoid our weaknesses. When we do that, we never progress or get any better."

—Jocko Willink

Eddie's relentless pursuit of leadership excellence extended far beyond the softball diamond. He was committed to infusing the wisdom he'd gained from his mentor, Mark Turner, into his role as a sales manager. These principles, once foreign to him, were now the cornerstone of his leadership.

In the realm of sales leadership, Eddie had always been celebrated for his remarkable strengths in sales strategy and fostering relationships. His ability to craft innovative sales strategies was renowned among his peers, and his knack for forging genuine connections with clients set him apart. He spent time coaching his team, offering invaluable insights into the art of relationship-centered selling that enhanced their ability to quickly connect with people.

Despite his strengths, Eddie was acutely aware of his limitations when it came to following up with his own team members. His struggles in this area had, on occasion, led to miscommunications, missed opportunities, and a sense of disarray among his sales team. Eddie was known for owning his mistakes; however, he needed a process to eliminate further issues in the future.

One glaring example of his limitations becoming evident was a missed deadline for one of his team members, Dave. Eddie had promised to provide Dave with additional resources for a critical presentation, but he failed to follow up. This resulted in Dave scrambling to prepare, and the presentation fell short of expectations.

In understanding his limitations and their impact on his team members like Dave and dedicating himself to enhancing his strengths, Eddie implemented new processes into his business. These processes enhanced his overall leadership effectiveness and provided a clear pathway to mitigate his limitations.

Integration into Eddie's business:

Personalized Sales Coaching: Eddie leveraged his sales strategy expertise to provide personalized coaching to his team members. He conducted individual coaching sessions, tailoring his guidance to each team member's unique strengths and areas needing improvement.

Streamlined Communication: To address his limitations in following up with his team, Eddie implemented a robust communication system. This system centralized team interactions and task management, ensuring important details and deadlines were never overlooked.

Follow-Up Protocol: Recognizing the importance of improving his follow-up within his team, Eddie introduced a comprehensive follow-up protocol. This protocol included regular check-ins, automated reminders, and meticulous tracking mechanisms to prevent missed opportunities and miscommunications.

Mentoring Relationships: Building on his relationship-focused approach, Eddie nurtured coaching relationships with each team member. This not only helped them professionally but also created an environment of trust and open communication.

Strategic Alignment: Eddie encouraged his team to engage in strategic planning sessions, aligning their individual goals with the organization's objectives. This strategic clarity enhanced team motivation and focus, with Eddie ensuring he followed up on their progress regularly.

These processes enabled Eddie to enhance his effectiveness, build trust with his team, and overcome his limitations. The sales team, especially Dave, flourished under Eddie's new processes and personalized guidance. The improved communication system minimized misunderstandings and miscommunications. Eddie's rigorous follow-up protocol turned missed opportunities into successful initiatives.

Perhaps the most striking transformation was the enhanced collaboration and trust within the team. Eddie's coaching relationships created an environment where team members felt heard and supported. The organization, once plagued by follow-up lapses, had transformed into a well-coordinated, efficient team. This resulted in increased productivity and elevated morale.

As Eddie observed the thriving sales team, he couldn't help but marvel at the journey he'd undertaken. His dedication to self-awareness and proactive leadership had borne fruit in the form of a high-performing sales team. Eddie had truly evolved into an exceptional sales leader, and he knew his journey was far from over.

CHAPTER 17

Bridges of Approachability

"The most important single ingredient in the formula of success is knowing how to get along with people."
—Theodore Roosevelt

Eddie and Lisa had taken the concept of approachability to heart, and it was beginning to transform the dynamics of the softball team. The players responded positively to the coaches' new approach, which emphasized open communication and genuine empathy.

One afternoon, after an exhilarating practice session where the players had shown dedication and improvement, Eddie and Lisa decided it was the perfect time for an informal team meeting. They wanted to hear from the players directly, to understand their experiences, concerns, and aspirations and to reinforce their commitment to being approachable leaders.

As the team gathered in a circle on the outfield grass, the coaches began the discussion. Lisa spoke first. "Alright, everyone, we're here today to hear from you. We want to know how you're feeling about the season, any challenges you've faced and what you hope to achieve. Your voices matter, and we're here to listen."

The players exchanged glances, initially unsure of how to respond. They had rarely been given such a platform to express themselves freely.

Eddie chimed in. "Let's start with this: what's something you love about playing softball on this team?" He looked at Maddie, the talented pitcher with dreams of playing college softball.

Maddie, normally reserved, took a deep breath and spoke, "I love the camaraderie. We support each other, win or lose, and it feels like a second family."

Eddie nodded, encouraging her to continue. "That's fantastic, Maddie. And what's something you think we could improve as a team?"

Maddie hesitated but then said, "Well, sometimes it feels like we're holding back on calling each other out for missing a play because we're afraid of being judged or criticizing others."

Eddie and Lisa exchanged knowing glances. They recognized this was precisely the kind of feedback they needed to hear. It was a turning point.

Lisa addressed the team. "Thank you, Maddie, for sharing that. It's important to us that you feel comfortable sharing and helping each other be successful. We are a team; pointing out missed plays and great catches alike makes us all better, it isn't to judge each other. We're here to help you grow, not just as athletes but as individuals too."

The floodgates opened, and one by one, the players began to share their thoughts. Some talked about their insecurities on the field, while others spoke about challenges they faced outside of softball. The coaches listened attentively, offering words of encouragement and solutions where they could.

After the meeting, the players felt a newfound sense of connection with their coaches. They saw them not just as authority figures but as mentors who genuinely cared about their well-being.

In the weeks that followed, the impact of their approachability became evident. The players began to approach Eddie and Lisa with questions about game strategies, technique improvements, and even personal advice. The coaches made an effort to be present for their players, responding to messages promptly and attending to their needs.

As a result, the team's performance continued to improve, and their bond strengthened. They started winning more games, not just because of their physical skills but also because of the trust and camaraderie they had developed.

Approachability had become the cornerstone of Eddie and Lisa's coaching style. It wasn't just a buzzword but a fundamental principle that had transformed them into leaders who inspired their team to reach new heights. The softball diamond had become a place where players felt safe to be themselves, to make mistakes, and to grow as athletes and as individuals.

CHAPTER 18

Inspiring Greatness

"Do not follow where the path may lead. Go instead where there is no path and leave a trail."

—Ralph Waldo Emerson

Eddie and Lisa had a growing sense of responsibility as they were surrounded by scraps of paper and inspirational quotes. Their team was heading into the biggest game of the season, and the weight of inspiring them fell squarely on their shoulders. They knew the right speech could elevate their players' spirits and drive them to victory.

Lisa took a deep breath, glancing at her collection of notes. "Eddie, we need to create a speech that not only motivates but also connects with each player personally. It has to be memorable."

Eddie nodded in agreement. "Absolutely, Lisa. The best speeches resonate with the heart and soul of each player. But how do we do that?"

They worked together based on Mark's guidance and the format he had used for motivational speeches throughout his years coaching lacrosse. The key elements for every speech were:

1. Personal Connection: Every great speech connects with the audience on a personal level. Eddie and Lisa knew they needed to acknowledge each player's journey, struggles, and successes.

2. Relatable Stories: Inspirational speeches often include relatable stories illustrating the message. The coaches thought about the pivotal moments in their players' lives and how they could use those stories to drive their message home.

3. A Vision of Success: They needed to paint a vivid picture of success, not just as a team but as individuals. What would victory look like, and how could they make it tangible for each player?

4. Empowering Language: Inspirational speeches are filled with empowering language. Eddie and Lisa knew they had to use words that ignited confidence and determination in their players.

5. Quotes and Anecdotes: They scoured books, movies, and famous speeches for memorable quotes and anecdotes that could bolster their message.

6. Call to Action: Every great speech ends with a call to action. What did they want their players to do once they left the dugout? How could they keep the fire burning?

With these elements in mind, they set to work. They began by reflecting on each player's journey, strengths, and contributions. They jotted down stories and anecdotes showcasing their dedication and resilience.

Lisa shared a particularly touching story about Maddie, the aspiring Duke pitcher. How she had overcome injury, worked tirelessly on her pitches, and inspired the team with her unwavering commitment. Eddie added anecdotes about players like Lilly, whose transformation from a shy and reserved second baseman to a passionate leader had been nothing short of remarkable.

They carefully selected quotes resonating with their team's spirit and goals. Quotes about teamwork, perseverance, and the pursuit of excellence found their way into the speech.

Eddie and Lisa then brought all these elements together into a narrative that would captivate their players' hearts and minds. They read the speech aloud to each other, tweaking sentences and adjusting the tone until it felt perfect.

As the day of the big game arrived, they gathered the team in the dugout. With the weight of their preparation and the power of their speech, they inspired their players to believe in themselves, to see victory not as a distant dream but as an achievable reality.

The players listened intently, their eyes filled with determination. Eddie and Lisa's speech was more than just words; it was a beacon of hope, a reminder of the extraordinary things they could achieve together.

Eddie and Lisa's Inspirational Speech before the Regional Finals

Eddie stepped forward, a quiet confidence in his eyes, and Lisa stood beside him, their unity a testament to their shared purpose. The team gathered around, eager faces turned toward their coaches.

"Team," Eddie began, "we've come a long way. Every early morning practice, every rain-soaked game, every moment of doubt, it's all led us to this point. The Regional Finals. The chance to prove ourselves, not just as a team but as a family."

Lisa added, "Each one of you has a story, a journey that brought you here. Think back to the first time you stepped onto a softball field. Remember the excitement, the nervousness, and the dreams you held in your hearts."

Eddie continued, "We've watched you grow, seen your dedication, your sacrifices. We've seen Maddie's unwavering commitment, Lilly's transformation into a leader, and the incredible spirit of every player on this team."

Lisa's voice filled with emotion. "Today, we stand at the precipice of something extraordinary. But remember, it's not just about the final score. It's about the journey, the battles we've fought, the bonds we've formed."

Eddie added, "Close your eyes for a moment and picture it. Picture the field and the crowd roaring with each play. Picture yourselves as champions, not because of the trophy but because of the heart and soul you put into every inning."

Lisa continued, "We believe in you, not just as athletes, but as remarkable individuals. As leaders on this field and in your lives beyond softball. Today, let's inspire each other to be the best versions of ourselves."

Eddie looked into each player's eyes. "As you step onto that field, know that you are not alone. You have a team that supports you, coaches who believe in you, and fans who cheer for you. Draw strength from each other."

Lisa concluded, "In the face of every challenge, remember the words of great athletes and leaders who came before us: 'You were born to be a player. You were meant to be here. This moment is yours. Believe in yourselves, and there's no limit to what we can achieve together.'"

With those final words, Eddie and Lisa watched as their players, hearts filled with inspiration, took to the field with renewed determination. The game that followed was more than a contest; it was a testament to the power of belief, unity, and the extraordinary ability to inspire greatness in one another.

That day, the team took the field with a newfound fire in their hearts, driven by a speech that had been carefully crafted to inspire and uplift. The elements they had learned—personal connection, relatable stories, a vision of success, empowering language, quotes and anecdotes, and a call to action—had combined to create a speech that would forever be etched in their memories.

CHAPTER 19

Integrity Prevails

"Honesty and Integrity is an important part of our character, my character."

—Nick Saban

The Regional Finals hung in the balance, the air thick with anticipation as the Blue Lightning entered the final inning trailing in a nail-biting 1-2 contest. The team desperately clawed for a breakthrough to keep their championship dreams alive. As Erin, sitting in the front row, and the rest of the spectators held their collective breath, the drama intensified with a runner on third and the winning run on second. Molly, the team's fastest player, took a lead at third, poised to steal and tie the game.

Eddie, donned in the Blue Lightning's colors, was the third base coach. His gaze, sharper than ever, dissected every nuance of the game with eagle-eyed intensity. The Blue Lightning's best hitter, Ellie, was at the plate. The opposing team's pitcher, a formidable force of skill and composure, now faced the pivotal moment where the weight of the entire season rested squarely on her shoulders.

The scoreboard displayed a daunting two outs as the pitcher wound up, delivering a pitch dancing dangerously close to the batter's box. The catcher, displaying agility, slid over to stop the wild pitch, with Molly on third, ready to exploit any opening. Molly, the team's lightning-fast catcher, recognized the opportunity and sprinted for home as the ball eluded the opposing catcher's grasp.

Molly, armed with her months of experience behind the plate, seized the moment, capitalizing on the chaos caused by the wild pitch. However, the real drama unfolded when the opposing catcher, engrossed in stopping the wild pitch, inadvertently obstructed the umpire's view. In the blink of an eye, the ball struck the batter's foot, sending it careening far beyond the catcher's reach. Molly, seemingly undeterred by the mayhem, slid into home, securing the tying run.

The Blue Lightning erupted in cheers, fueled by a concoction of adrenaline and jubilation, believing they had scored and tied the game. The opposing coach, irate and indignant, engaged in a heated argument with the umpires over whether or not the pitch hit the batter, which would send the scoring run back to third. This brought the field umpire toward home plate to mediate the escalating conflict.

In the midst of the commotion, Eddie recognized a golden opportunity to sway the umpires' decision. Struggling with an internal tug-of-war, torn between tying the game and keeping their best hitter at the plate and the principles he had instilled in his team, he approached the umpires. Silently and discreetly, he explained to the umpires his batter was limping and that in fact the ball had undeniably struck his batter, urging them to rectify the call. The umpires, initially bewildered, deliberated before announcing their final decision: the run didn't count, and the runner returned to third base while the batter took first.

Eddie, a sigh of relief escaping him, basked in the knowledge he had chosen integrity over coming closer to a win. However, as the tension subsided, a fresh wave of anxiety washed over him as his daughter, Riley, stepped into the batter's box. Eddie had taken on the coaching role not just for the love of the game but to deepen his relationship with Riley. Throughout the season, their connection had grown, but now, as she faced the pitcher with the bases loaded, down by one, and the weight of the team on her shoulders, Eddie's anxiety grew.

Erin was on the edge of her seat with the rest of the Blue Lightning fans, everyone hushed as Riley faced the first pitch, a high fastball, her Achilles' heel. She swung, and the resounding miss sent a ripple of unease through the crowd. Eddie couldn't contain himself and yelled, "She likes the high ones!" Riley smiled and knew it was his reference to *A League of Their Own* and her dad's way of saying "wait for your pitch."

Undeterred and confident from her preparation with Eddie for the Home Run Derby, Riley prepared for the next pitch. This time, the opposing pitcher threw a changeup. Drawing on hours of practice, Riley connected, sending a line drive through the gap over second base. The crowd erupted as Molly scored, and Sophie rounded third, Eddie waving her on home.

The centerfielder's throw met Sophie's slide, and in the dust, everyone strained their eyes for the umpire's call. The tension lingered before the umpire, with arms outstretched, declared Sophie safe. The Blue Lightning had done it—a 3-2 victory, propelling them to the State Finals.

Amidst the celebrations, Eddie knew this victory wasn't just about the scoreboard. It was a triumph of principles and a testament to the true meaning of leadership. The lesson in integrity at that pivotal moment would linger far beyond the softball field, shaping the character of each player.

In the midst of the celebrations, as Eddie embraced his daughter and waved to Erin in the stands, he understood their shared journey had not only strengthened their bond but had also imparted enduring lessons in resilience, integrity, and the unwavering pursuit of one's dreams. The victory, both hard-earned and ethically secured, etched an indelible memory of triumph in the Regional Finals—an experience that would resonate with the Blue Lightning players as they embarked onward to the State Finals.

CHAPTER 20

Golf Reveals Character

"Golf is a game of ego, but is also a game of integrity: the most important thing is you do what is right when no one is looking."

—Tom Watson

Following the softball regional finals, Eddie was excited to focus on work and one of the best events of the year for his clients, the company sponsored Pro-Am Golf Tournament. The event started on Tuesday evening at the clubhouse with a formal dinner with his sales team, top clients, and professional golfers.

Eddie decided to infuse a spirit of camaraderie and friendly competition among his sales team. Drawing inspiration from the principles of teamwork and goal-setting he had learned in coaching softball, Eddie proposed a unique challenge. The sales team would engage in a competition centered on achieving the most pars during the tournament.

The competition injected an air of excitement into their preparations for the tournament. Sales team members, usually accustomed to navigating the intricacies of deals and negotiations, found themselves strategizing and practicing their swings in unison. The prospect of friendly rivalry heightened their enthusiasm, turning the Pro-Am Golf Tournament into a platform where they could showcase not only their golfing skills but also their relationship skills with their clients. Each player from the sales team had contributed $20 to a side pot. The team member with the most pars for the day would take the pot and win bragging rights until next year.

As the morning got under way, Eddie found himself paired with Tony, a renowned pro golfer, and Tim and Brad, executives from two of his top Aerospace Technologies' client firms. Each of Eddie's sales team had their own foursome with their best clients. John, Eddie's top sales rep, was in the foursome behind him and took practice swings preparing for the round.

The tournament itself offered more than just a day of golf—it was a unique opportunity to foster camaraderie with clients, strengthen business relationships, and showcase the company's dedication to its clients. Eddie, known for his love of golf, approached the day with a hint of excitement and competitiveness in the air.

As the tournament unfolded, each foursome navigated the course, battling the challenges it presented. Eddie was having a good day on the course, making excellent shots and enjoying time with his clients.

As the tournament progressed, Eddie couldn't help but feel a sense of pride in his own performance. He had a strong day on the course and was content with how he had played. The final scores were posted on the board at the clubhouse, and the atmosphere buzzed with excitement.

Eddie believed in the spirit of the game and trusted everyone would play with integrity. However, as the evening unfolded and conversations about the tournament flowed, Eddie happened to overhear some chatter among his sales team.

In hushed tones, a couple of guys from his team were discussing John's round. Their words piqued Eddie's curiosity, and he moved closer to listen. One of them mentioned, "Did anyone else find it odd that John claimed so many pars today? I mean, I played in his foursome, and I don't remember him having that many."

Eddie discreetly asked the other members of his foursome about John's performance. To Eddie's dismay, the others confirmed his suspicions. John had exaggerated the number of pars he had achieved on the course, inflating his numbers to secure victory and win the pot.

Eddie's heart sank as he realized his top salesman had cheated to win the tournament. He felt a deep sense of disappointment and concern about the implications of John's actions for their professional relationship.

The next day, as Eddie reflected on the situation, he knew he couldn't let it slide. He arranged a private meeting with John. Eddie needed to confront his top salesman about the dishonesty and make him understand the gravity of his actions.

In the meeting, John, initially defiant, vehemently denied cheating. Eddie, however, remained resolute. "John," he said firmly, "integrity is fundamental to our professional lives. It's not just about this golf tournament; it's about the trust our clients place in us every day. When we compromise our integrity, we jeopardize everything we've built."

John's defenses began to crumble as Eddie emphasized the importance of honesty and ethical conduct.

"Eddie," John began hesitantly, "I have to admit, I might have made a mistake on my scorecard. It's not a big deal, though. I bought everyone drinks with the prize money, so we all had a good time."

Eddie appreciated John's admission, but it left him with a nagging feeling. If John was willing to bend the truth about a friendly golf tournament, could he be doing the same in more critical areas of his professional life?

A week later, as Eddie reviewed John's most recent expense reports, his suspicions grew. There were numerous questionable entries while John was on vacation, including extravagant client dinners, luxury entertainment expenses, and other items raising red flags. These expenses, all under the guise of fostering business relationships, seemed excessive and, in some cases, appeared to be fraudulent due to being outside of John's sales territory and while on vacation.

Eddie couldn't ignore the issues. The integrity of the company was at stake, and he knew he had to take action. With a heavy heart, he decided to report the matter to corporate HR for a formal review.

It was a difficult decision, one weighing heavily on Eddie's conscience. However, he believed it was crucial to uphold the company's ethical standards and ensure all employees, regardless of their position, adhered to the highest level of integrity.

As Eddie reflected on the situation, he couldn't help but draw parallels between the incident on the golf course and John's questionable business practices. Golf, he realized, was indeed a reflection of how one conducts themselves in life, and he was determined to uphold the principles of integrity and honesty in both realms.

In the end, Eddie's decision to confront the issue head-on, even when it was uncomfortable, served as a powerful lesson for the entire team about the value of integrity and the consequences of compromising it. It ensured they understood the importance of ethical conduct in their professional lives and reinforced Eddie's commitment to leading with authenticity and moral principles.

CHAPTER 21

The Authenticity Advantage

"It's important to be willing to make mistakes. The worst thing that can happen is you become memorable."

—Sara Blakely

The team thrived under Eddie and Lisa's coaching, focusing on extended practices as they prepared for the softball State Finals. However, as any team knows, challenges and conflicts can arise even in the best of times. It was during one of these moments the power of authenticity became abundantly clear.

Tensions ran high as the players pushed themselves to their limits. In the midst of a particularly grueling drill, a miscommunication between Riley and Lily led to a minor collision. No one was injured, but both players were visibly frustrated.

Eddie, who had watched closely, immediately halted the drill. He called Riley and Lily over to the sideline while the rest of the team took a much-needed water break. As the two players approached, their faces still flushed with frustration, Eddie could sense the tension in the air.

With a calm and empathetic tone, Eddie addressed them. "I saw what happened there, and I understand that it was a mix-up. Emotions can run high in practice, and sometimes, tempers flare. But let's remember, we're a team, and we're here to support each other. Lily, how did that collision make you feel?"

Lily took a deep breath and admitted, "I was frustrated because I thought Riley was going to move and let me catch the ball, but she didn't, and then we crashed into each other."

Eddie nodded. "Thank you for sharing that, Lily. Riley, how about you?"

Riley hesitated for a moment before responding, "I was frustrated too because I thought Lily was going to move out of the way, but she didn't, and I didn't know what to do."

Eddie appreciated their honesty. "It's okay to feel frustrated; we all have those moments. What's important is how we handle them. Riley, Lily, I want to apologize on behalf of both of you. I realize that I didn't provide clear instructions during the drill, and that contributed to the confusion."

Both players seemed surprised by Eddie's apology. They exchanged glances, and Lily said, "Thanks, Coach. Going forward, we will communicate and call out who has the ball to eliminate some of the confusion. We were both pretty upset, and it's good to know you understand."

Eddie smiled warmly. "Of course, I understand. We're all human, and we all make mistakes. The key is to learn from them and grow stronger as a team. Let's get back to practice, and remember, we're here to support each other, on and off the field."

As practice resumed, the tension hanging in the air began to dissipate. Riley and Lily shared a quick, genuine apology with each other, and the team rallied around them. What could have been a minor incident that festered into resentment had been diffused through authentic communication and an empathetic approach.

After practice, Lisa approached Eddie and said, "That was a great example of authentic leadership, Eddie. You didn't just address the issue; you owned up to your part in it and created a space for Riley and Lily to express themselves." Lisa continued, "It is wonderful to see how your relationship with Riley has transformed over this season. You both have a real connection that didn't exist before you started coaching."

Eddie nodded. "Thanks, our relationship has truly grown since I started coaching. The ability to be authentic with the players and especially Riley has really helped. Being real and vulnerable when it's necessary builds trust and fosters open communication. It's not always easy, but it's essential for our team's growth."

The softball team continued to flourish, not just in their skills but in their relationships with one another. They had learned authenticity was a strength, not a weakness, and it had transformed them into a cohesive and supportive unit both on and off the field. Eddie and Lisa knew these were the moments that truly defined their journey as leaders and mentors.

CHAPTER 22

The Fruits of Dedication

"If you want to be the best, you have to do things that other people aren't willing to do."

—Michael Phelps

Eddie had embarked on a coaching journey with his daughter's softball team, fully aware he was new to the coaching world. The early days were marked by uncertainty, a few missteps, and a profound learning curve. Yet, through every challenge he faced, he remained dedicated to the players and the sport.

As the team gathered for practice in the weeks leading up to State Finals, the atmosphere was charged with anticipation. The sun cast a warm glow on the field, and the gentle breeze carried the scent of freshly cut grass. It was a perfect day for softball.

Eddie, holding his clipboard, called the team together. The players formed a tight circle. Their faces bore the marks of countless hours spent under the sun, practicing their fielding, hitting, and base running. They were one united team.

Eddie began, his voice filled with a mixture of pride and gratitude. "Think back to when we first set foot on this field together. We were all newcomers, coaches and players alike. We didn't have the experience of seasoned teams, but we had something more precious: the determination to learn and grow together."

Lisa, her eyes shining with a sense of accomplishment, continued, "Through every challenge we faced, you never gave up. Whether it was a tough loss that tested your resolve or a thrilling victory that filled you with pride, you always came back to this field with the same unwavering dedication. As Derek Jeter once said, 'There may be people that have more talent than you, but there's no excuse for anyone to work harder than you do.' You all have truly embraced the value of hard work. This will benefit the entire team as we head to States."

The players exchanged knowing glances, recalling the moments of triumph and heartache they had shared. They had learned it wasn't just about winning games; it was about the bonds they had formed as a team and the personal growth they had experienced along the way.

Eddie spoke from the heart. "As your coaches, we've been inspired by your determination. Your willingness to listen, learn, and give your best effort in every practice and every game has made our job incredibly rewarding. You've shown that a strong work ethic and teamwork can overcome any obstacle."

Lisa nodded in agreement. "And now, we're heading to the State Championships not just as a team that has improved its skills but as a family that has supported one another every step of the way. Our work ethic and our unity have been our greatest assets, and they will continue to be as we face new challenges."

The players erupted into cheers, their voices ringing out with a shared sense of purpose and excitement. They knew their journey was far from over, but they were ready to face the State Championships with the same dedication and unity that had brought them this far.

The practice that followed was filled with intensity and camaraderie. Eddie and Lisa observed as their players honed their skills, but they also witnessed something deeper—the unbreakable bond that had formed between teammates who had grown together, both as athletes and as friends.

As they set their sights on States, the team was united not only by their shared journey and their unwavering work ethic but also by the knowledge they had evolved into a close-knit family. They were ready to face the competition, knowing their dedication, both as individuals and as a team, would be their greatest strength on the road ahead.

CHAPTER 23

Coffee and Conversations

"Communication is the most important skill any leader can possess."

—Richard Branson

On a sunny afternoon, Eddie found himself back at their favorite coffee shop, waiting for Mark. As he sipped his steaming cup of coffee, he reflected on the remarkable journey of growth he and Lisa had experienced as coaches and leaders. He knew this meeting with Mark would be another pivotal moment in their quest for leadership excellence.

Mark arrived with a warm smile, and they exchanged greetings. After catching up on recent events, Eddie leaned in, eager to share his newfound insights and seek further guidance. "Mark, you've been a beacon of wisdom on this leadership journey. The principles you've shared have made a profound impact on both coaching softball and at work as a leader."

Mark nodded appreciatively, his eyes reflecting the satisfaction of knowing he had made a difference. "Eddie, it's been a pleasure witnessing your growth and dedication to becoming a better leader. I'm here to help in any way I can. What's on your mind today?"

Eddie took a deep breath, eager to delve into the world of leadership once more. "We've been working diligently on understanding strengths and limitations, approachability, being inspiring, integrity, authenticity, and work ethic, just as you advised. And now, with State Championships approaching in a few weeks, I am interested in additional insights, particularly in the realm of communication."

Mark leaned forward, his eyes focused and intent. "Communication is indeed a cornerstone of effective leadership. Let me share a few key aspects that can elevate your coaching and leadership."

Understanding the Why: Mark began, "In any leadership role, whether as a coach or in your work, it's crucial to help those you lead to understand the "why" behind decisions and actions. When people understand the reasons behind what they're asked to do, they are more likely to buy into the vision and work with enthusiasm."

Eddie nodded thoughtfully, recognizing the power of providing context and meaning to their actions.

Clear Messaging: Mark continued, "Clear, concise messaging is another vital component. Avoid jargon or convoluted explanations. Speak plainly and directly. When your message is easily understood, it leads to better execution and minimizes misunderstandings."

Eddie envisioned how this could benefit both his coaching and his role at work. Clear communication could prevent confusion and foster unity.

Guidance on Expectations: "Setting clear expectations is a fundamental aspect of leadership," Mark emphasized. "Whether you're setting expectations for your team's performance on the field or your sales team's goals at work, make them specific, measurable, and achievable. This clarity helps your team know what's expected of them and how their success will be measured."

Eddie realized setting clear expectations could prevent ambiguity and ensure everyone worked toward the same goals.

Recognition and Feedback: Finally, Mark concluded, "Recognition is a powerful motivator. Don't underestimate the impact of acknowledging and celebrating your team's achievements, both big and small. Positive feedback reinforces desired behavior and performance."

Eddie thought about how recognizing effort and achievements could boost morale and encourage continuous improvement.

As their conversation continued, Mark shared practical examples and strategies for implementing these communication principles. To illustrate the importance of communication Mark began with a short parable about three bricklayers to illustrate the power of explaining the "why" behind actions. He leaned in, his eyes sparkling with enthusiasm, and began to share:

"The story of the three bricklayers is a timeless parable, rooted in an authentic tale from history. After the great fire of 1666, Christopher Wren, the renowned architect, was tasked with rebuilding St. Paul's Cathedral in London. One day in 1671, as Wren observed three bricklayers on a scaffold, he decided to strike up a conversation."

Eddie listened intently as Mark set the scene. He could almost picture the bricklayers on the scaffold, toiling away.

"Christopher Wren approached the first bricklayer and asked, 'What are you doing?'" Mark continued. "The bricklayer replied, 'I'm laying bricks to feed my family.' To the second bricklayer, Wren posed the same question and received a different response. 'I'm building a wall,' said the second bricklayer. But it was the answer from the third bricklayer that caught Wren's attention. With a gleam in his eye, the third bricklayer replied, 'I'm a cathedral builder. I'm constructing a grand cathedral, a place of worship for all, a sanctuary to honor the Almighty.'"

Mark paused, allowing the significance of the story to sink in. Eddie leaned back, reflecting on the different perspectives of the three bricklayers.

"The story," Mark continued, "teaches us many things, among them the power of a vision in gaining engagement from your team. Today, let's focus on the power of explaining the 'why' behind our actions. Imagine that Wren, intrigued by the third bricklayer's response, asked him, 'Why do you see yourself as a cathedral builder?'"

Eddie nodded, intrigued by the continuation of the story.

"The third bricklayer," Mark imagined, "responded with conviction, 'You see, Mr. Wren, every day as I lay these bricks, I'm not just building walls. I'm contributing to something much bigger than myself. I'm part of a team that's creating a place of worship, a sanctuary where people can find solace, connect with their faith, and seek guidance in times of need. Knowing that my work here helps others find their spiritual path gives my labor a deeper meaning.'"

Eddie's eyes lit up with understanding. "So it's about understanding how your work contributes to a larger purpose?"

Mark beamed. "Exactly, Eddie. When people see the bigger picture and understand why their efforts matter, it not only motivates them but also fosters a sense of fulfillment and commitment."

Eddie left the coffee shop that day with a profound appreciation for the guidance he had received from Mark. It was a reminder leadership wasn't a solitary path; it was a journey of continuous learning and growth.

CHAPTER 24

The Importance of WHY

"When we know WHY we do what we do, everything falls into place."

—Simon Sinek

Eddie had been on a journey of self-improvement as a leader, and the insights he gained from Mark Turner had profoundly influenced how he approached coaching his daughter's softball team. His newfound understanding of the importance of vision and explaining the "why" behind actions would enhance the way he led the young athletes.

As he drove to work the next morning, Eddie couldn't help but reflect on how these insights could also benefit his role as a sales leader. He thought about the recent successes with the softball team. Eddie had shared his vision of creating not just great softball players but confident, resilient, and empathetic individuals who could carry these qualities into their future endeavors. He had explained the "why" behind every drill, every practice, and every game.

The results had been astonishing. The girls were more motivated, dedicated, and driven to improve. They understood their hard work wasn't just about winning games but about personal growth and development. The vision had created a sense of purpose transcending the softball field.

But when Eddie arrived at the office, he realized there was a stark contrast. There continued to be a lack of enthusiasm and a sense of direction. His sales reps were focused on meeting their quotas, but they lacked a deeper understanding of why they did what they did beyond financial incentives.

Eddie decided it was time for a change. He shared his insights from coaching the softball team with his sales team and then introduced an innovative idea from Jennifer, who he had been coaching and working with on her career development.

"Team," he began, "I've been thinking a lot about our work and what motivates us. I've learned a valuable lesson from coaching my daughter's softball team. It's not just about hitting numbers or making sales; it's about the bigger picture—the 'why' behind what we do."

Eddie continued, "Just like our softball team, we need to embrace the vision we created. We need to understand that our work isn't just about meeting quotas. It's about making an impact on safety and protection across the globe. When we grasp the 'why' behind our actions, it becomes more than just a job; it becomes a mission."

Eddie then introduced Jennifer and her innovative idea. "Jennifer has been doing some incredible research to drive innovation. She approached me earlier this spring with an idea to expand our business into the automotive industry. She's done the groundwork, and I believe this could be a game-changer for us."

Jennifer, a passionate member of the team, took the floor and explained her findings. She showcased how their safety technology, originally designed for aviation, could be adapted and applied to automobiles, potentially saving countless lives on the road.

The team's skepticism transformed into enthusiasm as they realized the potential of this expansion. They now understood the "why" behind a broad strategic shift in their business model expanding beyond aerospace to include automotive. It was about safety, innovation, and making a lasting impact.

In the following weeks, Eddie and his sales team worked diligently to adapt their strategy for the automotive sector, guided by the vision of safety and innovation. They began explaining the "why" behind their actions to potential clients, illustrating how their technology could prevent accidents and protect lives in both aviation and the automotive industry. Enhancing safety and protection for travel on the ground and in the air.

Their expanded vision breathed new life into the team, igniting their passion and commitment. Eddie knew this was just the beginning of their journey toward making a global impact on safety and protection. But he was confident that by sharing the wisdom he had gained from coaching softball and embracing innovative ideas from his team members, they were on the right path to success, both on and off the field, or in this case, on and off the tarmac.

CHAPTER 25

Expectations: Every Player, Every Play

"Leadership is the art of getting someone else to do something you want done because he wants to do it."

—Dwight D. Eisenhower

With the State Championships just a week away, Eddie knew this practice session was pivotal. The team had come a long way, and they had a real shot at the title. As they gathered on the field, excitement and tension hung in the air.

"Okay, team," Eddie began, his voice filled with determination. "This is it, the big one. We've worked hard, and we've come so far. But now, we need to fine-tune our game to perfection."

The girls nodded in agreement, their eyes focused on their coach.

Eddie decided to address a specific scenario that had caused them trouble in previous games—the steal from second to third when Emma, the left fielder, didn't back up Sophia, the third baseman. He knew this situation could make or break a game, and they couldn't afford to leave anything to chance.

He called over Emma and Sophia for a demonstration. With a runner on second, Eddie simulated a play where the runner attempted to steal third. When Molly's, the catcher, throw to third was slightly off target, the ball sailed past Sophia.

Eddie paused the demonstration and turned to Emma. "Emma, I need you to back up Sophia every time, no matter what. It's not just her responsibility to cover third base; it's yours too. Your role as a left fielder doesn't end when the ball isn't coming your way. It's about supporting your teammates and being ready for any situation."

Emma nodded, taking the guidance to heart. She had sometimes overlooked this aspect of her role, thinking her primary job was catching balls hit her way.

Eddie continued, addressing the entire team. "Team, remember this: every player, every position, every play—everyone matters. If we're going to win the championship, we need to be a team in every sense of the word. It's not just about knowing your own role; it's about understanding and fulfilling the expectations for each scenario."

The girls nodded in agreement, realizing the importance of their roles. They were a cohesive unit, and they needed to work together seamlessly to secure victory.

The practice continued with a renewed sense of purpose. Eddie made sure to incorporate scenarios demanding teamwork and communication from every player. They practiced cut-offs and backup situations, ensuring each player understood their role in different game scenarios.

As the final whistle blew to end practice, the girls felt a newfound confidence in their abilities and the understanding of their roles. They knew if they encountered a steal from second to third in the championship game, Emma would be right there, backing up Sophia, ready to keep the play alive.

Eddie's coaching had instilled in them the importance of teamwork, expectations, and being there for their teammates, no matter the situation. With this vital lesson learned, they were more prepared than ever to face the challenges of the State Championship and, just maybe, bring home the title they had been working so hard for.

CHAPTER 26

The Power of Recognition

"Recognition is not just about rewards; it's about creating a culture of appreciation that inspires and empowers employees to excel."

—Simon Sinek

In the midst of planning for the State Championships Eddie was also planning a National Sales Meeting for Aerospace Technologies. Luckily the sales meeting was a week before the Championship game. After planning for the sales meeting for months, it was coming at a good time to get the team together due to the challenging experience of having to let John go due to a breach of integrity. Eddie's team had rallied together after John's departure and worked tirelessly to not only maintain their sales performance but to excel beyond expectations. James and Steve, his top two salespeople, had been instrumental in this journey, and Eddie was thrilled at the prospect of seeing them recognized at the meeting.

As the day of the meeting arrived, Eddie's excitement grew. He knew that his team's accomplishments deserved acknowledgment, and James' and Steve's dedication deserved special attention. Their consistent hard work and commitment to the company had not only contributed to its success but had also helped restore Eddie's faith in his team's integrity after the incident with John.

The meeting began with a buzz of anticipation in the room. Eddie and his team sat among colleagues, all waiting for their moment of recognition. Together, the CEO and the President, accompanied by a PowerPoint presentation, started to read off the list of top salespeople. The room was filled with a mix of pride and excitement as names were called.

However, as the presentation continued, Eddie couldn't help but feel disappointed. The CEO and the President seemed to rush through the list, mispronouncing names and barely pausing to individually acknowledge the achievements of the salespeople. Eddie knew how much effort his team had put into their work, and he had expected their recognition to be a highlight of the meeting.

As James and Steve's names were finally called, the moment felt underwhelming. Eddie had envisioned a standing ovation, or at least a heartfelt acknowledgment, but it was reduced to a brief mention on a slide in the presentation. It was clear the CEO and the President had not taken the time to truly understand the significance of their accomplishments.

After the meeting, Eddie found James and Steve and offered his heartfelt congratulations. He knew their accomplishments, which were a result of their dedication and hard work, deserved more recognition than they had received. As they discussed the meeting, Eddie realized how important true recognition and appreciation is to everyone, especially in front of their peers.

The following day, during Eddie's breakout session at the national sales meeting, he had a clear agenda in mind. He knew the previous day's disappointment in recognition was an opportunity to make a change, not just for himself but for his entire team.

As his team gathered in the conference room, there was a sense of anticipation. They had all felt a bit let down by the previous day's events, and they were eager to see what Eddie had in store for them.

Eddie took the stage and, with a genuine smile, began, "Good morning, everyone. I hope you're all feeling energized and ready for an exciting day ahead. Before we dive into our agenda, I want to start with the most important recognition of the meeting by acknowledging the incredible accomplishments of our team."

He invited James and Steve to join him at the front of the room. "These two outstanding individuals, James and Steve, have significantly exceeded their targets this year," Eddie continued. "Their dedication, hard work, and innovative approaches have made a great impact on our team's overall success."

James and Steve each took a turn sharing specific stories of challenges they had faced and overcame, as well as strategies that had worked exceptionally well. Their colleagues listened intently, applauding them for their achievements.

Eddie then shifted his focus to the rest of the team. "Recognition isn't limited to a select few. Each one of you has contributed to our team's success in unique ways. Whether it's consistently meeting your targets, providing valuable insights, or supporting your colleagues, your efforts matter."

He began to acknowledge individual accomplishments, sharing stories and highlighting the impact each team member had made. The atmosphere in the room transformed from anticipation to pride as each team member received their well-deserved recognition.

Eddie was careful to communicate not only what each team member had achieved but also why it mattered. He linked their contributions to the bigger picture, emphasizing how their efforts had contributed to the company's growth and, ultimately, to enhancing safety in the airline industry and the expansion into the automotive industry.

As the session continued, the team's mindset shifted. There was a renewed sense of commitment and camaraderie. They realized their hard work and dedication were valued and appreciated. The importance of recognizing and celebrating each other's achievements became evident.

In the spirit of transparency, Eddie also shared his commitment to improving the recognition culture within the team. He encouraged team members to express appreciation for each other's efforts regularly and openly, both in good times and challenging ones.

As the breakout session concluded, the team left the room with a newfound sense of pride and unity. They had experienced firsthand the power of recognition and understood its role in fostering motivation and commitment. Eddie's leadership had taken a significant step forward, aligning with Mark's insights on the importance of communication and recognition in leadership.

CHAPTER 27

The Dilemma

"A true leader has the confidence to stand alone, the courage to make tough decisions, and the compassion to listen to the needs of others."

—Douglas MacArthur

Eddie found himself facing a dilemma of significant proportions. As the national sales meeting concluded, he received a call from a large automotive prospect who wanted him to present to their executive team on Monday. The Softball State Championships were Saturday, Sunday, and the final game to be played on Monday. The same day as the most important meeting for his new expanded vision of dominating safety for the automotive industry.

His daughter and her teammates had worked tirelessly all season to earn their spot in the championship, and Eddie had been there every step of the way as their coach.

This automotive meeting was pivotal, a chance to pitch their safety technology to the automaker and potentially secure a game-changing distribution deal that could revolutionize their business.

Eddie had always been a dedicated and supportive coach to his daughter's softball team. He knew how much this championship meant to the girls, and they were counting on him to be there. On the other hand, the meeting with the automobile manufacturer was a career-defining opportunity that could benefit not only his company but also his team's financial security.

That evening, returning from the sales meeting, as Eddie entered his living room, he found Erin and Riley engrossed in a game of Clue, laughing and having fun. The scene was a stark contrast to the disconnected dinners of the past. Softball coaching had not only reignited Eddie's passion for the game but had also woven threads of connection back into the fabric of his family.

As he settled onto the couch with a sigh, Eddie could feel the eyes of both his wife and daughter on him. The thought of making a decision between the softball team and his sales team seemed daunting. The choice seemed to carry the echoes of Eddie's past struggles to balance work and family.

Erin, sensing Eddie's internal turmoil, looked up from the game and turned to him with a knowing expression. "What's going on, Eddie?" she asked, her voice a gentle invitation for him to share his thoughts.

Riley looked up, her eyes filled with curiosity and concern. "Yeah, Dad, what's going on? You seem stressed."

Eddie took a deep breath, his gaze shifting between Erin and Riley. The challenges he initially faced with a daughter absorbed in her phone and a wife entangled in local drama were now replaced with shared victories on the softball field. Coaching the Blue Lightning had not only brought joy to Riley but had also rekindled the spark between Eddie and Erin.

"Erin, it's the big championship game," Eddie began, his words carrying a mixture of excitement and conflict. "But, at the same time, there's this critical meeting at work. It's a dilemma, and I don't want to let anyone down."

Erin's gaze softened as she reached over to hold Eddie's hand. "Eddie, look at us. Softball brought us back together as a family. Riley's happier, and so are we. You've been there for her and for us in ways I hadn't imagined. This decision is about more than just a game or a meeting. It's about the choices we make as a family."

Riley nodded in agreement, her concern evident. "Dad, the softball team needs you. You've made a difference, not just for me but for all the girls. We've come so far, and this championship means a lot to us. You can't miss it."

Eddie felt a swell of emotion as he looked between his wife and daughter. Softball had become a bridge that spanned the gaps in their relationships, and the upcoming choice would be a testament to the transformative power of a game, a family, and the delicate balance between them.

"I know," Eddie replied, his voice laced with conviction. "Softball has given us something more than wins and losses. It's given us a chance to rebuild, to be there for each other. I can't let go of that, Erin. I can't let go of what we've found in the game and in each other."

Erin smiled gently. "Eddie, remember the lessons you've learned about leadership from your meetings with Mark.

You've told me how crucial it is to create a vision, communicate it clearly, and set expectations. Maybe it's time to reflect on your own vision for yourself, our family, and your career. Take a day to think about what's important and also how it aligns with your own beliefs and vision for you as a leader. We will support you in whatever you decide."

Eddie considered Erin's words. It wasn't just about being physically present; it was about having a vision for himself, being transparent, setting expectations, and helping the softball team and his sales team see what was possible as he led by example.

As Eddie contemplated the decision, he knew this moment marked a pivotal juncture not just in his coaching and leadership journey but in the intricate dance of work, family, and newfound connections that defined his household. The upcoming choice would be a testament to the transformative power of a game, a career, a family, and the delicate balance between them.

CHAPTER 28

Leading with Purpose

"A man should never neglect his family for business."
—Walt Disney

Eddie found himself facing an internal struggle on where to place his priority, family or work. The girls' Softball State Championship Game and a critical meeting with one of the largest automobile manufacturers in the country were scheduled for the same day. His daughter's softball team had made it to the State Championships, a culmination of months of hard work and dedication. On the other hand, the meeting with the automobile manufacturer was a career-defining opportunity for Eddie's company, and the potential benefits were enormous.

Eddie wrestled with this decision. He knew whatever choice he made would have significant consequences for both his family and his career. He recalled the lessons he had learned from Mark about leadership and the importance of maintaining a balance between work and personal life.

As he reflected on his personal mission as a leader, Eddie realized it was rooted in creating new leaders within his team. It was about fostering a work environment where individuals could grow, take on more responsibilities, and thrive. Jennifer had originally brought the idea of expanding into the automotive industry. She was highly capable, but she lacked experience in leading critical meetings, even though he had been working with her for this type of career opportunity.

Eddie knew that this was an opportunity to live out his mission and demonstrate effective leadership in action. He decided to prioritize family and the growth of his team members. Eddie had been working with Jennifer on preparing to present together at the auto manufacturer once the executives aligned on a date. She was inexperienced yet understood the market and was growing in her ability.

Eddie reached out to Jennifer and explained the situation. He shared the importance of the meeting with the automobile manufacturer and the potential it held for their company's future. Eddie offered to continue coaching and support Jennifer, providing guidance, insights, and resources to ensure the meeting's success. Jennifer was initially surprised by Eddie's decision but deeply grateful for the opportunity.

In Eddie's weekly sales call, he addressed his team, his voice reflecting a blend of resolve and sincerity. He began by expressing his genuine excitement about the upcoming State Championships, underscoring the significance of the event in his daughter's life. He shared his realization that, over the years, he had sometimes placed his work ahead of personal moments that truly mattered. He admitted he had almost made the same mistake again with the conflicting automobile manufacturer meeting. Eddie then explained he had decided to prioritize his family and his commitment to developing leaders within the team.

With heartfelt clarity, he stated, "Our team's success isn't solely about closing deals or hitting numbers; it's also about personal growth, family values, and creating leaders. I believe in each of you, and I'm confident that Jennifer, whom I've been mentoring and the person who initiated this new distribution opportunity, is the best person to represent us in the meeting. This is an opportunity for us all to grow and learn from each other. I'm proud to be a part of a team that understands the importance of balance and development, and I hope this choice reflects our commitment to these principles."

Eddie's words resonated with his team members, reaffirming the company's culture of balance, personal growth, and teamwork.

Eddie and Jennifer spent the next few days preparing for the meeting, with Eddie imparting his knowledge and expertise. He emphasized the importance of creating a vision, understanding the "why" behind their technology, and effectively communicating it to the auto manufacturer.

Eddie's decision to prioritize family and leadership had a profound impact on his team. It reinforced the values of work-life balance and nurturing talent within the organization. The decision increased engagement and commitment from the team as they believed Eddie was living the principals of an effective leader in creating more leaders.

CHAPTER 29

The Big Day

"The mind is the limit. As long as the mind can envision the fact that you can do something, you can do it, as long as you really believe 100 percent."

—Arnold Schwarzenegger

After a few tough games to qualify for Monday's finals and the day unfolded, the tension grew. Eddie found himself in an unprecedented dual event, torn between his daughter's championship game and Jennifer's automotive meeting. Both events were moments of truth for him and his team.

As Eddie stepped into the championship finals on that Monday, his heart was torn between hope and fear. The game unfolded with each inning, a gripping saga of highs and lows keeping everyone on the edge of their seats. In the decisive final inning, with tension thick in the air and the outcome hanging in the balance, Maddie stood confidently on the pitcher's mound. Throughout the game, she had displayed remarkable strength and determination, overcoming every obstacle thrown her way. Now, with the bases loaded and the tying run just a breath away, all eyes were on her. The weight of the championship rested squarely on her shoulders, a daunting responsibility for someone so young.

The crowd held its collective breath as the count ran full—three balls, two strikes. The batter had a formidable reputation, and everyone knew she could turn the game around with one swing of the bat. Eddie watched Maddie, her face focused and determined. She wound up and delivered the pitch of her life—a changeup that danced gracefully across the plate.

The batter swung with all her might, but the ball eluded her, clipping the corner of the strike zone. The umpire's emphatic call of "Strike three!" reverberated through the stadium. Maddie had done it—she struck out the final batter, securing the State Championship for her team. The crowd erupted in cheers, and Eddie couldn't have been prouder.

Simultaneously, miles away, Jennifer found herself facing the biggest challenge of her career in the automotive meeting. The room was filled with executives and decision-makers from the industry giant. Jennifer had spent days preparing for this moment, and as she began her presentation, she channeled all her knowledge, passion, and the guidance she had received from Eddie.

She spoke eloquently, presenting the "why" behind their technology as the solution the automotive company needed. She answered questions confidently, addressing concerns with finesse, and demonstrated a deep understanding of the industry's needs. Jennifer's presentation was not just about selling a product; it was about building a partnership based on trust and innovation.

As she concluded her pitch, there was a moment of silence that seemed to stretch for eternity. Then, one by one, the executives began nodding in approval. The atmosphere in the room shifted, and the tension eased. The automotive executives saw the value in what Jennifer offered. By the end of the meeting, they had not only expressed their intention to work together but had already initiated the contract negotiations.

The softball game was so intense and Eddie was so focused on the girls' performance, he forgot to check his phone to see how Jennifer's meeting was going. When he finally reached down to check his messages, he saw a text from Jennifer, "We won the deal!" His girls' victory and Jennifer's success in the meeting seemed almost poetic, a testament to the importance of family, mentorship, and the unwavering pursuit of excellence.

As he embraced his daughter in celebration of their state championship, Eddie couldn't help but feel an overwhelming sense of pride. In that moment, he knew he had made the right choice, one that had allowed both his family and his team to achieve remarkable victories. It was a day he would forever cherish, a day when leadership, family, and dreams had all come together in perfect harmony.

CHAPTER 30

Leadership Excellence

"Good leaders build products. Great leaders build cultures. Good leaders deliver results. Great leaders develop people. Good leaders have vision. Great leaders have values. Good leaders are role models at work. Great leaders are role models in life."

—Adam Grant

As the sun dipped below the horizon, casting a warm, golden hue over the coffee shop where Eddie and Mark had often met, the two men sipped on their steaming cups of coffee. Eddie was eager to share not only his professional successes but also how his evolving leadership philosophy had transformed his relationship with his daughter and her softball journey.

"Eddie," Mark began, a warm smile on his face, "it's truly remarkable how far you've come since we began exploring the leadership principles."

Eddie's eyes gleamed with gratitude as he nodded appreciatively. "Mark, I can't thank you enough for the guidance and mentorship you've provided. It's made a profound impact on both my coaching and my career."

As their conversation flowed, Eddie couldn't help but share the intertwined stories of success that had unfolded in both the world of softball and his professional life, all thanks to Mark's wisdom.

Eddie began, "Applying the leadership principles you shared with me has been nothing short of amazing. I started with creating a vision—a vision that extended beyond the softball field. I wanted those girls to not only excel as players but also grow into confident and compassionate individuals."

Mark interjected with a knowing smile. "Vision sets the foundation for everything."

Eddie eagerly recounted how being people-focused had played a pivotal role. "Helping to guide young players to expand their minds and see a bigger future for themselves became my mission. Take Maddie, for instance. She was a good player with aspirations to do well during the season; with a few conversations, we were able to identify a longer term goal of playing at the college level, which refocused her dedication to sports and also academics."

Mark leaned in. "Appreciating the power to help others recognize what is truly possible, that's the essence of great leadership."

Eddie went on, touching upon the significance of emotional intelligence. "During high-pressure moments, like a crucial game, I helped the girls manage their emotions. It made all the difference. Lily, our second baseman, overcame her nerves to deliver a game-winning hit."

Mark chuckled in agreement. "Emotions play a pivotal role in leadership and performance."

With a smile, Eddie recounted how the girls began to inspire each other, celebrating small victories and fostering a culture of encouragement and resilience. "It wasn't just about winning; it was about growth and support."

Mark leaned back, thoroughly impressed. "Eddie, it's great to see how these principles have breathed life into your coaching and your life."

As their conversation meandered, Mark and Eddie continued to exchange stories and insights, emphasizing the transformative power of effective leadership. Eddie knew he owed a tremendous debt of gratitude to Mark. His mentorship hadn't just improved his coaching and work performance—it had deepened his connection with his daughter. It was a testament to the enduring influence of these leadership principles.

Mark recounted his experiences as a CEO, where he had steered his company through challenging times. "Understanding my own strengths and limitations was critical. It enabled us to make strategic decisions and adapt to shifting circumstances."

Mark's stories seamlessly intertwined with Eddie's narrative, creating a rich tapestry of leadership insights that spanned the realms of softball and business. Together, they marveled at how these principles had the power to elevate not only performance but also the human connections that lay at the heart of it all.

As Eddie and Mark sipped their coffee, their conversation flowed effortlessly from one leadership principle to another, a testament to the depth of their mentorship. Mark was eager to hear how Eddie had applied these principles to his work as well.

"Eddie," Mark inquired, "how have these leadership insights translated into your work with the sales team?"

Eddie's eyes twinkled as he embarked on another part of his journey. "Mark, you remember Jennifer, one of my sales team members. She had this brilliant idea about expanding our business into the automotive industry. It was an aha moment—the kind that stems from vision. I realized that our vision needed to extend beyond just selling technology for airline safety. It was about making an impact on safety and protection in the air and on the ground."

Mark nodded in approval. "That's what vision does—it propels us forward."

Eddie continued. "With our success in the aerospace industry expanding into the automobile industry, I have been charged with leading sales across both segments, creating an opportunity to promote Jennifer to lead sales for the new automobile division. Jennifer was instrumental in this expansion. She had the drive and innovation and has developed into a strong leader. And I must say, it has been a game-changer."

Mark leaned in, intrigued by the growth within Eddie's team. "Creating new leaders is what leadership is all about."

With enthusiasm, Eddie expanded on his leadership lessons. "I realized that to truly lead a team, I needed to set clear expectations. Just like I coached my daughter's softball team, I coached my sales team on their roles. Whether it was someone in left field or someone responsible for a key client, they needed to understand the importance of their contributions."

Mark interjected thoughtfully, "Expectations provide clarity and direction."

Eddie couldn't help but share a recent success story from work. "We had a high-pressure situation during a client presentation. The client had concerns, and we had to respond effectively. It was a moment to apply emotional intelligence. I reminded my team to stay calm, listen actively, and address concerns empathetically. And you know what? We secured the deal."

Mark nodded approvingly. "Emotional intelligence is a superpower in leadership."

Eddie's storytelling continued, highlighting the significance of approachability. "Creating an environment where team members feel comfortable coming to me with questions or ideas was crucial. Just like my softball players, my sales team needed to know they could trust their leader."

Mark agreed, reflecting on his own experiences. "Approachability fosters trust and an open exchange of ideas."

Their conversation took another turn, delving into the importance of inspiring a team. "Before our regional finals," Eddie recounted, "I gave an inspiring speech to the girls. It boosted their morale and motivated them to give their best. Similarly, before our crucial automotive meeting, I crafted an inspiring story of what success would mean for us and for the company. It spurred my team on."

Mark smiled, recognizing the value of inspiration. "Inspiration fuels action and commitment."

Eddie rounded off his tales by emphasizing the significance of authenticity. "Being authentic with my sales team, just as I was with my softball players, built trust. It showed them that I valued their contributions and respected them as individuals."

Mark nodded, acknowledging the power of authenticity. "Authentic leaders forge deep connections."

As they concluded their coffee-fueled conversation, Mark and Eddie shared a deep sense of satisfaction. Eddie had internalized the leadership principles, applying them with precision both on the softball field and in the dynamic world of sales leadership. The story of his journey served as a testament to the transformative power of effective leadership—a lesson he had learned from an invaluable mentor who believed in the potential for growth and excellence in every endeavor.

As Eddie prepared to leave the coffee shop, he glanced around the warm, familiar space that had witnessed countless conversations with Mark. It was then, for the first time, his eyes fell upon a sign hanging proudly on the wall. Eddie realized why Mark had brought him to this specific coffee shop for all their meetings. The sign had the name of the coffee shop **"Batter's Glove Café"** with a specific meaning for each letter of the café.

B: Be people focused.

A: Approachability and authenticity.

T: Transparent and ethical conduct.

T: Teamwork and collaboration.

E: Emotional intelligence.

R: Recognition.

S: Strengths and limitations.

G: Guiding principles and work ethic.

L: Leadership.

O: Openness to personal development.

V: Vision for a better coffee experience.

E: Excellence and commitment to quality coffee.

A smile crept across Eddie's face as he realized these qualities were more than just words—they were the guiding principles that had transformed his coaching, his leadership at work, and his life as a whole. With a renewed sense of purpose, Eddie stepped out into the world, carrying these invaluable lessons with him and determined to share them, just as Mark had shared them with him.

EQUIPMENT FOR SUCCESS

Effective Leadership Principles

Client—Character—Communication

Client: Your Clients are Your Team Members

Vision: A leader articulates a compelling vision, aligning team members toward a common goal, and continuously communicates progress and adjustments.

Vision for Career: A leader actively supports team members in defining and pursuing their career aspirations, providing opportunities for growth and advancement.

Development: A leader fosters a culture of continuous learning and development, providing resources, mentorship, and feedback to nurture individual and team growth.

Emotional Intelligence: A leader demonstrates empathy, self-awareness, and effective communication, creating an inclusive environment where emotions are acknowledged and managed constructively.

Character: Your Personal Character

Strengths and Limitations: A leader is aware of their strengths and limitations and transparently communicates them to the team, fostering an environment of honesty, trust, and collaboration.

Approachability: A leader maintains an open-door policy, actively listens to concerns, and fosters an environment where team members feel comfortable seeking guidance and feedback.

Inspiring: A leader leads by example, exhibiting passion, optimism, and resilience, and motivates others through clear communication, recognition, and support.

Integrity: A leader upholds ethical standards, acts with transparency and honesty, and holds themselves and others accountable for their actions.

Authenticity: A leader cultivates trust by being genuine, sincere, and consistent in their words and actions, building authentic connections with team members.

Work Ethic: A leader sets high standards for themselves and their team, demonstrating dedication, perseverance, and professionalism in pursuit of organizational objectives.

Communication: Ability to Share Your Message

Understanding the "WHY": A leader communicates the purpose and significance behind tasks and decisions, fostering buy-in and commitment from team members through clarity and alignment.

Clear Message: A leader communicates with clarity, simplicity, and relevance, ensuring messages are easily understood and effectively convey expectations and objectives.

Guidance on Expectations: A leader sets clear expectations, provides regular feedback, and offers support and resources to help team members meet and exceed performance standards.

Recognition: A leader acknowledges and celebrates individual and team achievements, demonstrating appreciation and reinforcing desired behaviors and outcomes.

Great leaders create more leaders.

SMART Goals are an effective framework for setting and achieving objectives. SMART stands for Specific, Measurable, Achievable, Relevant, and Time Bound.

S **Specific**: Your goal should be clear and specific, answering the questions of who, what, where, when, why, and how. Vague goals are harder to achieve because they lack clarity. By making your goal specific, you'll know exactly what you're working toward.

M **Measurable**: You should be able to track your progress and determine when you've reached your goal. Including specific metrics or milestones helps you gauge your progress and stay motivated. Measurable goals provide a way to objectively evaluate your success.

A **Achievable**: Your goal should be realistic and attainable given your resources, skills, and timeframe. It's important to set goals that stretch you but are still within reach.

R **Relevant**: Your goal should align with your overall objectives and be meaningful to you or your organization. It should be relevant to your values, priorities, and long-term plans.

T **Time-bound**: Your goal should have a deadline or timeframe for completion. Setting a deadline creates a sense of urgency and helps you prioritize your tasks.

ADDITIONAL RESOURCES:

Dr. Kevin McGarry, the founder of McGarryLeadership and CEO of Leading360, is a distinguished leadership consultant specializing in executive coaching and organizational development. Renowned for his advocacy of effective leadership, authentic communication, and the cultivation of high-performing teams, Dr. McGarry offers transformative workshops and coaching sessions.

Through Leading360, Dr. McGarry provides a global leadership platform, empowering leaders to assess their skills and elevate their effectiveness through actionable strategies.

Explore our offerings:
- Consulting services
- Speaking engagements
- Free resources
- Podcasts

Visit our website at www.mcgarryleadership.com to:
- Access research on Effective Leadership.
- Listen to leadership podcasts.
- Work directly with Dr. Kevin McGarry.

Discover more at www.ileading360.com to:
- Engage in a Personalized Leadership Assessment.
- Access resources for enhancing leadership effectiveness.
- Subscribe to the Leading360 monthly newsletter.

For inquiries regarding leadership, sales, and team-building programs grounded in *Lead with Purpose* principles, reach out to Dr. Kevin McGarry:

Phone: **860.255.8414**

Email: kevin@mcgarryleadership.com

Online: www.mcgarryleadership.com